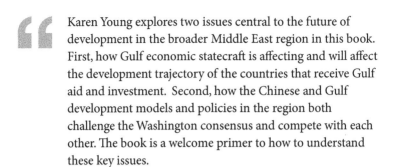

Karen Young explores two issues central to the future of development in the broader Middle East region in this book. First, how Gulf economic statecraft is affecting and will affect the development trajectory of the countries that receive Gulf aid and investment. Second, how the Chinese and Gulf development models and policies in the region both challenge the Washington consensus and compete with each other. The book is a welcome primer to how to understand these key issues.

F. GREGORY GAUSE, *Texas A&M University, USA*

This meticulously detailed and extraordinarily timely analysis of economic statecraft in the context of the Gulf Arab States sheds valuable light on the political motivations and policy tools that are reshaping patterns of aid, development, and investment strategies across the Middle East and North Africa at a time of enormous volatility and great uncertainty in the global economic and energy landscape.

KRISTIAN ULRICHSEN, *Rice University, USA*

In *The Economic Statecraft of the Gulf Arab States*, Karen Young investigates a little understood, but fundamental shift in South-South economic relations: the increasing deployment by Gulf oil monarchies of large-scale overseas capital in the wider Middle East and beyond, for both commercial and political purposes. Perceptive and rich in detail, the book documents how state-directed cross-border capital flows bypass the Bretton Woods system and its rules-bound framework, creating new avenues of influence for Gulf rulers and new challenges for established Western powers. At least in the wider Middle East, the GCC's new tools of economic diplomacy rival and sometimes outshine those of China in scale and strategic importance.

STEFFEN HERTOG, *London School of Economics, UK*

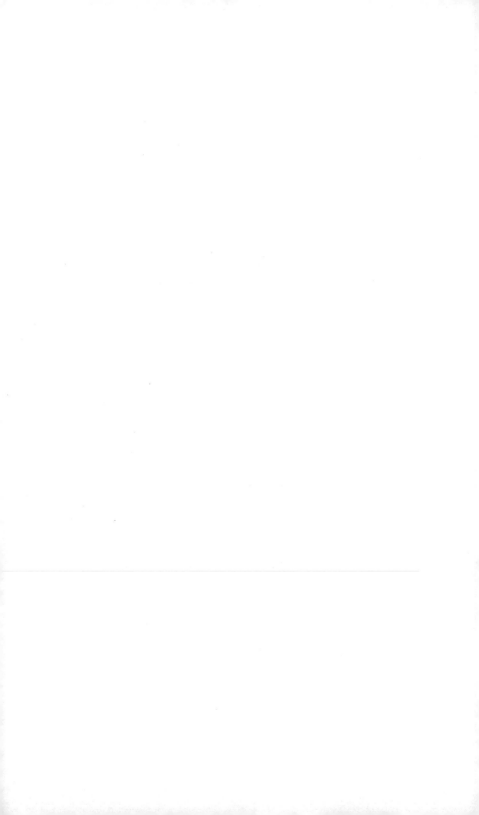

THE ECONOMIC STATECRAFT OF THE GULF ARAB STATES

The MEI Policy Series aims to inform policy debates on the most pressing issues that will shape the future of the Middle East. The series publishes manuscripts that provide cutting-edge analysis and recommendations to policymakers in the Middle East and to international actors as they work toward solutions to some of the most searing problems facing the region.

Seeking to contribute to policy debates that will influence the Middle East in the future, the MEI Policy Series promotes innovative and incisive work that focuses on issues that cut across the various countries of the region and span the areas of politics, culture, economics, society, the state, climate, health, gender and any other issue that meets the above policy impact criteria.

THE ECONOMIC STATECRAFT OF THE GULF ARAB STATES

Deploying Aid, Investment and Development across the MENA

Karen E. Young

I.B. TAURIS

LONDON • NEW YORK • OXFORD • NEW DELHI • SYDNEY

I.B. TAURIS
Bloomsbury Publishing Plc
50 Bedford Square, London, WC1B 3DP, UK
1385 Broadway, New York, NY 10018, USA
29 Earlsfort Terrace, Dublin 2, Ireland

BLOOMSBURY, I.B. TAURIS and the I.B. Tauris logo are trademarks of
Bloomsbury Publishing Plc

This edition published 2023 by I.B. Tauris, an imprint of Bloomsbury Publishing

Series design by Charlotte Daniels
Cover image © VideoFlow/Adobe Stock

A catalogue record for this book is available from the British Library.

A catalog record for this book is available from the Library of Congress.

ISBN: HB: 978-0-7556-4665-4
        PB: 978-0-7556-4666-1
        ePDF: 978-0-7556-4667-8
        eBook: 978-0-7556-4668-5

Typeset by RefineCatch Limited, Bungay, Suffolk

Series: Middle East Institute Policy Series I MEI

To find out more about our authors and books visit www.bloomsbury.com
and sign up for our newsletters.

For Alma and Beatrice

CONTENTS

ILLUSTRATIONS

Figures

Tables

ACKNOWLEDGMENTS

This book was possible with a grant from the Smith Richardson Foundation to fund the data collection on foreign direct investment and to support research assistance from Laila Hanandeh at the American Enterprise Institute. I am grateful to Laila for her professionalism, diligence, and organization skills in compiling the data and figures for this book, formatting the manuscript, and helping with copy edits. Dany Pletka supported the idea of the project from the beginning of my tenure at AEI and was instrumental in the grant writing process. Kori Schake further supported the research project when she joined AEI in early 2020. I moved to the Middle East Institute in May 2021 and finished the manuscript for publication, already under engagement with IB Tauris. IB Tauris and MEI then separately agreed to form a joint imprint and invited my book to be a first title in the series. This research did not receive any funding from MEI or any foreign or US government sources. The work is mine alone and I bear responsibility for the findings and, of course, any errors or omissions.

There are many people who have prompted my thinking and conceptualization of this project, in my time at the Arab Gulf States Institute in Washington (AGSIW) from 2015–2018, and at the American Enterprise Institute (AEI) from 2018–2021. The manuscript was submitted in January 2022. Some early conceptualizations included a workshop at the Gulf Research Meeting in Cambridge in 2018 that led to a collaboration with Taimur Khan in an edited volume *The Gulf States and the Horn of Africa* published by Manchester University Press in 2022, looking specifically at the role of the UAE in the Horn, in investment and financial intervention, as well as in infrastructure and securitization through ports. At AGSIW and at AEI, I developed three public datasets that informed this book. One, the Gulf Economic Barometer at AGSIW, tracked economic policy shifts, debt issuance, and the beginning of the wave of liberalization reforms from 2015 with the collapse of oil prices through 2018. At AEI, I created the Gulf Economic Policy Tracker, focusing on the policy response across labor markets, foreign investor rights, debt issuance, and social policy to the sharp decline in oil prices in late 2015 to 2020. Also at AEI, I created the Gulf Financial Aid and Direct Investment Tracker, to quantify and delineate the financial support from the six Gulf Cooperation Council states to a set of nine recipient case countries across the Horn, North Africa, the Middle East, and Pakistan. I have presented pieces of this project and its data related to aid and foreign investment in a number of settings over the last three years, in publications with Bloomberg, Al Monitor, AEI and MEI, and in workshops or speaking engagements with the European Council on Foreign Relations, Center for New American Security, Gulf Research Centre, the Brookings Institution, the US State Department, and in university lectures.

With the Russian invasion of Ukraine in February 2022 and a mounting uncertainty around global energy supply and the continuity of a system of economic order, based on principles of liberalism and open markets, this book seems even more relevant. The emergence of new powerful economic actors in the Gulf, with their own ideas about development as a process and the deployment of wealth for political purpose is certain to change the world. How the United States continues to engage with these states, and how the Gulf states respond, will be a bellwether to a descent into a bifurcated global political economy.

INTRODUCTION

Master Developers of the Gulf

On a hot day in Mogadishu in April 2018, a private jet landed at the capital's airport loaded with nearly $10 million in cash, a form of direct government support from the United Arab Emirates to the army of Somalia, intended for the military and trainees, according to the UAE (Salman & Aamir, 2018). Upon arrival, the cash was seized by local authorities (Cornwell & Browning, 2018). The image of a botched case of suitcase diplomacy, in which the receiving government accused the sending government of meddling in internal affairs, was an unfortunate reminder of the informality and corrosive effects of some aid and financial intervention.

But more importantly, this episode also represents an outdated mode of financial aid and intervention from the Gulf Arab states that is still real, but at the fringes of a much larger and consequential trend line. A few million dollars in a suitcase is miniscule compared to Gulf state capacity for official development assistance, state-led foreign direct investment, and the use of central bank deposits and in-kind oil and gas transfers to a widening sphere of recipient cases. The Gulf Arab states are development actors in a class of their own, often able to deploy sums of direct support that international financial institutions and international organizations cannot match in either investment or aid. The fact that these states may also rely on old patterns and norms of patronage and purposeful largesse to leaders and rival groups is a remnant of weak aid and foreign policy institutionalization, but also a tell-tale sign of the continued hierarchy and agility of Gulf intervention. It's from the top. It has discretionary budget limits. And it can make or break the leadership and economic ambitions of its beneficiaries.

This book is a study of a shift in the politics and finance of development from one centered in the institutions and ideas of the post-World War II global political economy to the emergence of South-South economic ties and the rise of authoritarian or state capitalism as an alternative model of development. This is a study of the economic statecraft of the Gulf Arab states, specifically the deployment of aid, investment, and direct support from some of the wealthiest petrostates of the world to their surrounding sphere of influence within the Middle East, Horn of Africa, and West Asia. The study is based on a three-year data collection project funded by the Smith Richardson Foundation, the Gulf Financial Aid and Direct Investment Tracker, available at the American Enterprise Institute. The dataset includes official development assistance, foreign direct investment (from both state-owned/government-related and private entities) and other forms of direct finance, including central bank deposits and oil and gas in-kind assistance from 2003 to 2021. The sending countries include all six of the Gulf Cooperation Council states (Bahrain, Kuwait, Oman, Qatar, Saudi Arabia, and the United Arab Emirates) and a set of aid and investment recipient case countries (Djibouti, Egypt, Ethiopia, Israel, Jordan, Lebanon, Oman, Pakistan, Sudan, Turkey, and Yemen).

By grouping both official development aid, cash, and in-kind transfers and foreign direct investment together, we get a broader picture of financial intervention and a broader understanding of some of the mechanisms of support that state actors have at their disposal. The old ways of understanding development finance relied on limited tools of international financial institutions, i.e., using balance of payment support (via the IMF) or concessionary finance and lending (via the World Bank) and the private flow of capital (foreign direct investment or private bank loans). New ways of understanding development finance prioritize the developmental state as an actor replicating its own patterns and reliance on state-owned investment vehicles or sovereign wealth funds, discretionary aid, and informal transfers of products like oil and gas, along with direct cash support. The trend line of authoritarian development models is surging, notably from China's Belt and Road Initiative (BRI), but also deployed by the Gulf Arab states.

These new models of development finance, aid, and intervention include distinct institutional designs and ideological bases. For the United Arab Emirates, Saudi Arabia, and Qatar, the preference for state-led and often state-owned development is a strategic priority in the energy sector, a mechanism for domestic economic growth and consolidation of wealth among leadership and ruling families. Exporting that agenda as a foreign economic policy tool continues all of the domestic benefits, while also affirming broader regional political goals—whether that is undermining certain movements or giving a hand to like-minded autocrats. This pattern is not so different from the norms of exporting democratic capitalism model advocated by Western powers for most of the second half of the twentieth century.

For most of the post-World War II era, the United States believed that its model of investment and development represented not simply the sole model of building aspirational democratic capitalism, but one that was underpinned by global institutions and unfettered by competition. That is no longer true, and while the United States still has the capacity to offer a transformative global investment and development model, it neither does so aggressively nor does it appreciate the reality of growing competition in that sphere. Emerging models of state-led growth, market intervention, and preferential treatment of state investment within market institutions are challenging the preference for democratic capitalism as a source of ideological influence and a prescriptive for growth. We see these new models gaining traction outside of multilateral development institutions like the International Monetary Fund and World Bank, as new states vie for opportunities as agents of finance and development across emerging markets. China is of course a leader in this effort through its BRI policies, but other small states with deep pockets have staged equally disruptive interventions.

The Gulf Arab states are especially active now as agents of development finance. Across the Middle East and Horn of Africa, it is the Gulf Arab states—Saudi Arabia, the United Arab Emirates, and Qatar in particular—that are the new master developers, capable of financial intervention at and beyond the scale of traditional international development institutions. They are remaking the markets of potential political allies, new destinations for their energy products and their post-oil investment future. The role of the Gulf states as master developers is essential to understand within a broader shift in sources of capital investment and new ideas about state-building and economic development most often attributed to Chinese influence and its South-South development agenda. While China has dominated in other regions, its investments and interventions in the Middle East are limited geographically and sectorally. When compared with American and European private investment efforts, China spends less and creates fewer jobs in most of the Middle East,

North Africa, and West Asia (OPEC, 2018). Indeed, the Gulf states have higher capital expenditure and create more employment across the Middle East and North Africa than China—and that's not counting remittance flows, aid, financial intervention such as central-bank deposits, and in-kind oil and gas transfers (Young, 2018b). China is active as a regional investor and contractor where private capital doesn't want to go—places like Iran, Syria, and, to a degree, Turkey (Newlines Institute, 2020). One notable exception is the United Arab Emirates, where Chinese investment and contracts have surged since 2016. This skews the data and inflates China's reputation as a regional investor and source of capital. The view that China is the largest investor in the Arab region overlooks the fact that Beijing has invested inconsistently over time, and picks and chooses its engagement in the broader region, from Morocco to Pakistan. The assertion also fails to mention that the Gulf states are now a major and often more important source of foreign direct investment in that same geography.

In 2021, the most important source country of outgoing foreign direct investment within the Middle East and Africa was the United Arab Emirates (Financial Times Ltd., 2021). In 1970, the United Arab Emirates did not exist as a state, but was rather a loose configuration of emirates under tribal leadership, under the treaty protection of the British. There was little infrastructure in roads, schools, or public health, and there was no unified national defense system until the early 1990s. The UAE was of interest to the British not as a source of natural resources to plunder (although oil was discovered in the 1960s, production did not accelerate until after state formation), but rather as a land base to protect the more important asset of open sea lanes through the Persian Gulf. Finance and capital flows have changed considerably since 1970 in the Gulf states. Since independence, the model of state-led growth has coincided with the accumulation of wealth from oil and gas export revenues. But equally important are ideas about consolidated national ownership, centralized economic planning, and a drive for expansion and connectivity to regional and global markets. The Gulf states see their security and their economic survival dependent on getting their energy products to market, but also sustaining relationships with consumers and governments in those markets. Aid, investment, and statecraft are the tools of that relationship management.

Emerging markets or developing economies from Africa to the Middle East now have some interesting choices in development finance partners.

Where the money comes from matters. First, sources of development finance create institutional consequences in the recipient state. Second, the deal-making of development finance creates political alliances that transcend the development transaction, and in many cases, can reinforce patronage networks and personalistic politics. Third, the efficacy of project delivery and its long-term viability, whether infrastructure investment in utilities or social infrastructure in health and education, depends on governance, competition, and the mutual benefits of rule-based markets.

Development usually entails the construction of utilities for electricity, clean water, and access points, whether in roads, seaports, or airports that enable trade and the connectivity of people. Infrastructure is the physical evidence of a developmental state in action. Much of the demand for infrastructure investment in emerging markets is being met by predatory lending and recycled petrodollars, rather than market-based solutions. Using the broadest definition of infrastructure, the world spent $9.5 trillion on all types of asset classes in 2015, equivalent to 14 percent of global GDP, according to McKinsey research (Woetzel et al., 2016). The world needs to invest $3.7 trillion in economic infrastructure annually through 2035 to keep pace with projected growth, and more than 60 percent of the investment needed will be in emerging markets. But, to meet that finance demand and to tap the development potential of the Middle East, Eastern Europe, Latin America, China, and beyond requires political and ideological leadership. Ideas about how best to finance growth, and how to direct it for inclusive growth across society, are political. The lasting impact of the role of Gulf states' directed aid and investment in its near abroad, from the Horn of Africa through the Levant, remains to be seen, but the early evidence supplied in this book points to sectoral concentrations in foreign direct investment, politicized interventions that tip the scales in divided polities, and a focus on returns that track directly to Gulf strategic priorities in food security, port access, and market share in providing energy products (from oil to solar power) and their petrochemical derivatives.

This book is organized to make the case that ideas about development—how best to generate economic wealth and how best to share it across a polity to improve human productivity, health, and connectivity—are essentially political choices, informed by norms, history, and informal institutions. And ideas about development exist and emerge within moments of the global political economy. The ability to dominate a narrative about growth, progress, and competition has a lot to do with shifts in the production and demand of natural resources. The rise of the Gulf states occurred in tandem with the dominance of the United States in the post-Cold War, and the US security commitment to the Gulf allowed these states to focus on domestic economic development and resource extraction more than external security threats or foreign policy outreach.

The emergence of the Gulf Arab states as proactive interventionists in regional politics and economies coincides with a sense of American disengagement from the Middle East for a reason. As does the parallel development of ideas of state-led and authoritarian capitalism between China and the Gulf. Abdulkhaleq Abdulla has described this emergence of the Gulf states on the international and regional political map as "the Gulf moment" (Kawas, 2018). I have described the movement toward financial, political, and military intervention in the region by the Gulf Arab states as a process that includes a firm calculation of cost-benefit analysis, but also of return on investment for state entities (and ruling families), in financial terms as much as—if not more than—in political influence (Young, 2013).

The book proceeds in the following order. The first chapter offers a historical view of development finance institutions and prescriptive ideas of growth, originating in the post-war order. In the literature on economic development, there are clear arguments for the symbiotic relationship between growth and more open political systems and guarantees of property rights and the enforcement of rules. Since the 1990s, with the economic liberalization of China and a more outward-focused foreign economic policy agenda, new development banks and access to development finance products have changed, opening the way for alternative ideas and processes in South-South investment and growth ties. The entry of the Gulf Arab states in this trajectory is a factor of the accumulation of tremendous oil and gas wealth in the "magic decade" between 2003 and 2014, the earthquake of the Arab Spring in 2011, and the internationalization of Gulf foreign policy goals. This is the context of the theory of development meeting the emergence of Gulf economic statecraft.

Chapter Two is a study of the political economy of the Gulf in efforts to diversify from oil and gas rents, to monetize state hydrocarbon resources, and to rebuild national oil companies into global energy powerhouses. This is the context of how the Gulf Cooperation states have envisioned and turned development ideas into action in their own domestic environments. Levers of control from the consolidation of power of ruling families, state support to incubate nascent national industries, and determination to transform along with the changes in global energy demand and sources work together to inform a Gulf development strategy, with some important variation within these resource-rich states. The second chapter also explains the synergy of Gulf-China ambitions in the Horn of Africa and West Asia, across high population and high growth markets to create markets for full-stream energy products, from petrol to petrochemicals and plastics, as a way to capture new markets and customers and form political alliances for access. For China, domestic labor markets and financial institutions have relied on outreach to developing economies. For the Gulf, outward investments and financial support have their own regime survival justifications.

Chapter Three gets to the empirical data collected for this study, which continues in a series of case comparisons in Chapters Four and Five. The book includes six explicit recipient case studies, selected in pairs to represent larger themes in Gulf financial aid and intervention. The case selection includes variation in the size and scale of recipient economies, levels of need in their access to aid and development finance, history of conflict and sanctions. The cases also vary in the investigation of sending countries, and the role of intra-Gulf rivalry and approaches to economic statecraft. The larger proprietary dataset for the project is available on the American Enterprise Institute website with additional cases, including Turkey, Israel, Lebanon, and Jordan.

The book uses the evidence of Gulf state financial aid and intervention, its comparison to what other states and international financial institutions provide, and the results in the destination case country. In Chapter Three, cases of Gulf financial intervention in Egypt and Ethiopia demonstrate the capacity of competing forms of financial support to achieve foreign policy goals. Egypt's receipt of aid and investment flows from Qatar between 2011 and 2013, and then the UAE and Saudi Arabia from 2013 to 2020 illustrate this trend, in its political nature and also in the deep capacity Gulf states have for financial intervention. More than $80 billion went to Egypt from the Gulf in the form of central bank deposits, foreign direct investment, and state-sponsored support in this decade, 2011–2020. The coordination of multilateral support, in Egypt's debt package from the International Monetary Fund is also novel in this period, as it entailed Gulf commitments of support. In Ethiopia, we see the extensive use of sovereign wealth funds to allocate foreign direct investment as a political commitment of the UAE. The chapter explains why Ethiopia is a target of interest, and how these commitments were often difficult to uphold, given the structural barriers of Ethiopia's financial system and its regulatory hurdles (a closed banking system), and a difficult domestic political transition under Prime Minister Abiy Ahmed.

Chapter Three describes the two largest cases of the study in terms of financial intervention and also in terms of the size and potential of these economies, with their large populations and attractive foreign direct investment profile. In some ways, these two cases are the best-case scenario of South-South development finance and intervention, with support from external actors (including the IMF and Western governments). But in both of these cases, we see the highly politicized nature of Gulf state financial intervention, privileging favored domestic political actors as well certain industries and sectors for investment that generate returns arguably more for the Gulf than for the local economy. The chapter examines data on job creation, and comparative data on foreign direct investment from the Gulf states alongside that of China, states of the European Union, the United Kingdom, and the United States. The comparative analysis shows the rise of the Gulf states in this period between 2003 and 2021 as sources of finance and support, but also their ability to surpass other sources of support.

Chapter Four examines how Gulf and Chinese financial intervention work sometimes in synergy and sometimes in competition in recipient states. The co-investments in the energy sector by both Gulf and Chinese state oil companies is one example. In Oman and Pakistan, we see the Chinese Belt and Road Initiative in its full ambitions, but also the overlap of Gulf energy transition goals and some intra-Gulf rivalry, a part of the sub-regional dimension of Gulf foreign policy. The Omani case also illustrates the difficulty developing countries find when they are in need of external finance, and how traditional sources of loans and debt issuance in private markets are often not available, making state-led development finance solutions more attractive. In Pakistan, we see the corporatization of Gulf financial intervention, using Gulf state-owned oil companies as sources of investment, but also strategic positioning of assets within an energy value chain, from refineries to petrochemical facilities. Likewise, the ability to reward and award states with access to their own mechanisms of revenue generation is indeed a tool of economic statecraft. The Abu

Dhabi National Oil Company awarded the Pakistani government oil company a concession to drill for oil in the UAE in the summer of 2021, in a tender that saw many international oil companies surprised to see competition from a much smaller state-owned firm (Saadi, 2021).

Chapter Five poses the problem of aid and investment flows to countries in crisis, either in civil war or under sanctions and excluded from private international capital flows. The chapter examines the cases of Sudan and Yemen, both recipients of significant Gulf financial aid and intervention, and both in dire need of assistance. The Gulf states have had extraordinary influence and ability to maneuver within these two political economies, at times also contributing to conflict, humanitarian crisis, and poor governance. These cases also shed light on the challenge of enticing private investment in post-conflict and active-conflict environments, and the performance of state-directed investment. As a counter-example, the new financial ties between Israel and the UAE and Bahrain after the Abraham Accords in 2020 provide a case of how state-led investment, even in strong economies, may not be able to animate and accelerate equal interest from private sector investors.

Chapter Six is an effort to square the circle, offering some policy recommendations for the Gulf Arab states and the United States, acknowledging the current power and resources deployed from the Gulf and the clear need for new sources of finance for development across the Middle East and Horn of Africa. In the field of renewable energy, for example, there are clear areas of shared interest ripe for collaboration. For governments interested in the promotion of rules-based economies and liberal markets, there might be ways to combine development resources and private capital to work as an alternative to state-led solutions, or at least work in partnership with them. For those governments seeking aid and financial support from the Gulf, there are reasons to proceed with caution and to try and create leverage on the ground, in promoting skilled job training and worker benefits to build local capacity.

As a whole, this book offers a comprehensive, data-rich examination of the deployment of economic statecraft by a set of increasingly important and powerful state actors across a diverse geography in the Middle East and Horn of Africa. Economic statecraft is using economic means to achieve foreign policy ends. It is economic policy deliberately formulated to promote the foreign policy goals of the state (Baldwin, 1985). But there is a difference between foreign economic policy and economic statecraft. As Benn Steil and David Litan argue, economic statecraft applies economic means to ends which may or may not be economic, whereas foreign economic policy encompasses means which may or may not be economic in the service of economic ends. Such that trade sanctions imposed on a country in order to persuade it to halt a weapons program would qualify as economic statecraft, but not foreign economic policy. But suspending diplomatic ties with a country—a non-economic intervention—in order to object to its import barriers would qualify as foreign economic policy, but not economic statecraft (Litan & Steil, 2006). In the United States, discussions of economic statecraft usually center on the use of sanctions, or punitive measures to elicit a change in policy of an adversary (Drezner, 2021). But economic statecraft is also about economic conciliatory measures and incentives with a policy objective in mind for the recipient state, but also with a domestic strategic objective.

The story of the rise of the Gulf Arab states in the global economy is a story of a new geopolitics of finance and aid, but also of an emerging multipolarity and competition between systems of order and ideas about how best to organize state and economy. The introduction of alternative sources of aid and investment for developing countries—those struggling to meet the basic needs of their citizens, from access to water and electricity to education and employment—is both a benefit and a risk. It is a risk for those who advocate for and anticipate a return to American unipolarity and a dominance of market-based ideas for economic development, and to the primacy of traditional Western aid and multilateral lending and balance of payment support through the Bretton Woods institutions. But the addition of new sources of aid and finance might also be a benefit to the United States and its Western allies, to have new partners with financing resources to bring to the development agenda.

The challenge is shaping a shared agenda when the central ideas about the appropriate role of the state in economic growth are not aligned. Added to that is the sense of threat of authoritarian capitalism, and concerns of how resource distribution may consolidate patterns of repression, inequities, and lack of mobility for marginalized groups. But the development agenda established at Bretton Woods also had its favorites and never achieved a level playing field in terms of access to finance, especially during the Cold War. Similar ideological battles exist for the Gulf states in their deployment of foreign aid, investment, and financial intervention.

There is now a heated debate in US foreign policy on the appropriate role of the United States in its ambitions abroad in efforts to shape the global environment in its security and economic interests. For many across Republican and Democrat party lines, the urge is for a doctrine of American restraint, less interventionist in its use of military force and posture globally, less vocal in its promotion of democracy and defense of free markets, and more reliant on a "diplomatic toolkit" (Ashford, 2021). But what the American restraint advocates often fail to understand is how developing countries see the coming American disengagement, especially in the Middle East. The United States is pulling up the ladder not only on its commitments to a security umbrella across the Gulf and wider Middle East, but also foreign aid and the facilitation of access to capital. It is not clear that absent the security leverage, whether governments will encourage the other kinds of reforms and institutionalization specific to the openness of markets and accessibility of finance that the US has promoted. Even diplomatic toolkits and economic statecraft need hard power behind them.

The abandonment of the defense of the liberal order sounds overwrought, but in practice this will occur in more subtle ways. For example, an American presence and pressure means more than boots on the ground. It has also included training and oversight within central banks in the Middle East, to encourage private banks to "know their customers" and discourage money laundering and illicit finance networks, to expand lending to smaller businesses that might compete with state-related entities, and to encourage regulation that gives women equal access to financial services. An American-friendly business environment has also meant regulations that welcome foreign investment, allow foreign ownership of property, equities and firms. It has meant access to credit markets, and encouragement of bond issuances, which in turn require a great deal of government and firm-level disclosures of their budgets and operations. The United States and its citizens, financial firms, and public companies certainly benefit as well—as arrangers of debt issuance and as investors in regional debt products, often through pension funds and index funds.

We expose our own financial markets and services to a creeping authoritarianism when we facilitate capital flows and investment opportunities for state-owned and linked firms in authoritarian governments. We literally feed the businesses of state repression. Matt Pottinger has argued that it is possible to "stem the flow of US capital into

China's so-called military-civil fusion enterprises" (Pottinger, 2021). Without US capital markets, most of China's successful technology companies would not exist, because they would not have gotten off the ground. Decoupling from China, however, seems nearly impossible, and certainly would come at a high cost to the United States. The idea of a flowering of economies across the Global South without access to US capital markets starts to look like a very bipolar global economy, and eventually, one that may see the diminution of the United States in size and scale. Moreover, the impact to human freedom, economic mobility, and innovation would be devastating. Otherwise we need to provide alternatives, to stay in the game, and to demonstrate the advantages of linkages with the United States and its institutions of capitalist democracy.

Beyond ideology and politics, there is the shared impact of the climate crisis and the impending energy transition, which will shape the areas of cooperation and competition between the Gulf states and China. The Russian invasion of Ukraine in late February 2022 accelerated an energy crisis already in motion and has deepened the need for energy security and a reality check on the role of traditional oil and gas exporters in the global economy. It is not a question of *if* the Gulf states will continue to play a role in global energy security, but *how* and *where* they will do so. And their importance will not stop with oil and gas. Where Gulf state energy giants will devote resources for market share and dominance in the next phase of their own diversification process could create enormous opportunity for some states, as a site of hydrogen power, solar power, or petrochemical production for plastics that construct the renewables sector, for example. The Gulf diversification agenda into renewable energy sources (especially in the promise of green hydrogen) may also see their continued dominance and wealth creation. But just as easily their interest and ability to intervene in a widening sphere of influence could be halted, sending a set of new partners into financial crisis. What is certain is a reconfiguration of the available sources of development assistance and finance and a wide divergence of prescriptions for growth.

1 POLITICAL ECONOMY OF DEVELOPMENT FROM BRETTON WOODS TO AUTHORITARIAN CAPITALISM

In studying the political economy of development, politics often entangle with economic theory prescriptions for growth. Every country faces specific challenges and exists within concentric domestic, regional, and international spheres of influence. Despite more than a century of academic inquiry into the question of wealth and disparity between political systems, there remains a great deal of debate about the best ways to meet a shared goal of ending poverty. Notwithstanding the acrimony in academic and policy circles, however, the general trend of poverty reduction and access to finance achieved through the Bretton Woods system has demonstrated incredible progress.

The logic of development assistance after World War II has been based on a consensus that open markets are best able to deliver growth, and that leverage from international financial institutions to encourage liberalization and rule of law can nudge (or force) governments to make better economic choices. That advice has been largely successful, as the World Bank reports, at creating "remarkable and unprecedented progress in reducing extreme poverty over the past quarter century. In 2015, more than a billion fewer people were living in extreme poverty than in 1990. The progress has been driven by strong global growth and the rising wealth of many developing countries, particularly in the world's most populous regions of East Asia and Pacific and South Asia" (The World Bank, 2018). The opening of China and the ignition of economies in South Asia, driven by a global consensus on the power of liberalization and access to finance, has changed the world. However, it did not happen in a vacuum. American ideas about markets inspired China's liberalization and then facilitated it through access to capital through international financial institutions that America helped create. In fact, China's access to World Bank loans, and more broadly, the advice and access to institutions of a global liberal economic order, have enabled and accelerated its growth (Dhue, 2019).

Yet, the quest for economic growth is "elusive," as William Easterly (2001) describes it, because there is a great deal of variation across culture, history, natural resources, and geography in countries that are wealthy and in those that are poor. Economic development is not just dependent on capital flows or capital accumulation, nor is aid a panacea and a one-stop solution to poverty (The World Bank, 1998). Moreover, debt relief as a form of foreign aid does little if political behavior (and a reliance on borrowing or printing currency) continues along the same lines as before. Even "enlightened leadership" cannot create economic growth on its own. As new work by Joseph Stiglitz and others has acknowledged, human capital is also essential to economic growth, as is a culture of learning and knowledge production, which often includes risk-taking and entrepreneurship (Stiglitz & Greenwald, 2014). As a particular challenge to China, Li et al. (2017) and other scholars are now more willing to engage the causal power of softer institutions, from education policy to media, to credit the role of ideas in encouraging and sustaining economic growth.

Other questions on the appropriate role of the state in economic development continue to generate debate between public choice theorists (as in the work of James Buchanan and Robert Tollison) and development economists (such as Joseph Stiglitz and Karla Hoff) who see a more active role for the state (Buchanan & Tollison, 1984; Stiglitz & Hoff, 2001). However, there is some consensus that institutions matter, as the pioneering work of Douglas North (1990) demonstrated, as do ideas and informal institutions or patterns of behavior and beliefs that establish "ways of doing business." In this sense, the normative power of rule-based economic institutions and the politics that support them can have enormous effects on development outcomes, whether the goals are poverty alleviation or improving basic access to social infrastructure like health and education.

Political scientists have also struggled to determine the effects of democracy on economic growth and if there is a causal relationship between economic development as conducive to initiation and consolidation of democracy. Seymour Martin Lipset's[1] work, along with the classic modernization formulation of "no bourgeoisie, no democracy" of Barrington Moore, predicated the growth of wealth and a middle class to support democratic development (Lipset, 1959; Moore, 1966). However, later work by Guillermo O'Donnell and others questioned how some forms of economic development and industrialization, particularly managed by the state, could create alternative political institutions that leaned (or twisted) toward authoritarianism (Moore, 2015). State-led growth and the East Asian miracle in the 1990s, then China's economic liberalization and rise in the 2000s, have certainly diminished the explanatory power of economic growth as an indication of future democratization (The World Bank, 1993).

Which brings us back to trying to understand how economic growth, powered by internal or external forces, has a number of institutional and political pathways. Outside forces—whether bilateral aid, multilateral lenders, or more direct intervention as an act of economic statecraft by an ally or adversary—can redirect a path toward prosperity or a path back to isolation and poverty. In addition, in the meantime, interventions of either kind may tear down the political green shoots of accountability and competition. The tendency for rent-seeking behavior to extract uncompensated value from others without contributing to productivity can be rampant when external sources of aid and investment have few strings attached (Kreuger, 1974). More recent scholarship by John Gerring, Peter Kingstone, Matthew Lange, and Aseema Sinha has questioned the durability of democracy as an indicator of continued economic performance, not for the survival time but more for the ability of democracies to create patterns of behavior in policy consensus and enacting successful policy reform (Gerring et al., 2011). This suggests, again, that the quality of institutions and the practice of competition of ideas and consensus-building in democracies best support sustained economic performance.

Breakthrough work by Daren Acemoglu and James Robinson (2012) aptly explains why and how economic growth occurs and what political institutions best support it. Their conclusions are essential to understanding the risk of "hot money" or personalistic transfers of development aid and direct investment support in fragile political economies in Africa and the broader Middle East. Their theory rests on the nature of institutions—meaning the rules, both formal and informal, that govern economic and political life. Certain types of economic infrastructure such as property rights or enforcement of contracts create incentives for investment and innovation. Those institutions that can create a level playing field where both local citizens and foreign investors can use their skills and talents are "inclusive economic institutions." On the other hand, there are "exclusive economic institutions" designed by purpose to extract resources from the society for the benefit of a few. These economic institutions are sustained by political institutions concentrated in ownership. Their takeaway is clear—you cannot succeed economically if you do not get your politics right; but there is no formula for getting politics right. Nevertheless, we can identify methods of statecraft and intervention that make economic growth less politically stable and less likely to engender participatory politics. It is also possible to empirically track and evaluate how development aid and financial intervention from new authoritarian sources impacts the domestic politics of recipient states. We can identify points of vulnerability and track records of performance.

Understanding the incentives of economic statecraft for those states willing to extend aid, foreign direct investment, loans and credit, as well as direct cash support to central banks or in-kind products of oil and gas complicates a very one-sided view of the development agenda (Harris & Blackwill, 2016). It is not just the fault of the recipient state if its economic policy choices fail to deliver; it is also a collaboration of unequal and sometimes divergent state interests. In the case of intervention during a political transition from authoritarianism, or a transition following civil war or conflict, the risks of development aid and investment become increasingly fraught, with the likelihood of conflict recurrence fueled by an influx of resources that can be hoarded, and local-level grievances that seek retribution after conflict, as the work of Paul Collier has demonstrated (The World Bank, 2003).

The literature on the political economy of development and democracy has made important contributions to our understanding of why there is such variation in economic performance across regimes and geographies. Researchers have also established a number of variables seeking to measure the strength of the relationship between democracy and economic growth. All of this work, however, assumes certain power dynamics of the international system and its institutional capacity to engage as agents of development finance and sources of economic advice. The system is what has changed. The Bretton Woods, post-colonial world of development has shifted; particularly in the assumption of American leadership and hegemony in a liberal economic order.

In fact, a recent essay in the *Financial Times* argues that of the three main alternatives of the twentieth century, liberalism, fascism, and communism, only liberalism remains (Harari, 2019). Yet, new populist movements and authoritarian resurgence challenge key elements of liberalism. Defining liberalism has also become about selective elements, rather than an understanding of how its economic and political tenets work together. Liberal economics uphold free markets, the value of contracts and enforcement mechanisms, and insists on the efficacy and mutual benefit of free trade. Political liberalism upholds free elections, freedom of expression, and appreciates the value of institutions in facilitating cooperation between countries. As Yuval Noah Harari argues, the preference of many developing countries now is the "buffet" approach to liberalism, to pick and choose among its elements, rather than seeing the benefit of combining its political and economic tenets.

Debates on rising inequality and the threat of terrorism both provide support to alternative visions of political and economic governance. Those visions are less concerned with international norms, multilateral engagement, rule-based markets, and individual freedoms. They justify intervention and repression on the grounds of stability; while their deployment of wealth, earned through natural resources and state-controlled industry, allow them to advance a moneyed soft power with tangible commitments of cash, infrastructure, and investment.

While many analysts are focused now on the size and scale of Chinese investment, and some are awakening to the role of other financial interventionists in emerging markets, there is not a comprehensive study of how these new actors fit into a revolution. There is an upheaval in our understanding of the political economy of development and the logical impacts we can expect to find in governance and support for democracy.

China and the Gulf Arab states are actively engaged as agents of development finance for their own financial and political interests and with very little engagement with multilateral financial institutions, official development agencies, or private finance. Work by AEI scholar Derek Scissors has been essential in tracking and establishing the scope of Chinese financial aid and intervention in emerging markets. Baker Mackenzie estimates that Chinese projects associated with the Belt and

Road Initiative will have a value of $350 billion by 2022, while there are already more than 1,700 BRI projects completed or in development (Baker McKenzie, 2017).

The phenomenon of Gulf Arab state support to a widening sphere of influence in the Horn of Africa, Middle East, and Pakistan is only growing in intensity. The author's own work has been at the forefront of efforts to understand this regional deployment of economic statecraft (Young, 2013, 2014). Moreover, since 2011, the exercise of economic statecraft, whether through direct commitments of financial support, promises of foreign direct investment, or in-kind oil and gas transfers, have been plentiful and from sources on both sides of the GCC political divide. As of yet, no scholarship has connected this trend of the Gulf states to the activities of China, and to the broader deficit of liberal economic policy approaches toward emerging market governance and finance needs. The author's work has posed this dilemma most recently in an article in the context of the COVID-19 pandemic and how development finance choices for recovery matter even more for their institutional consequences and reordering of global power centers (Young, 2020c).

Since 2018, Saudi Arabia and the United Arab Emirates have committed $6 billion (each) to Pakistan, $3 billion to Ethiopia, $10 billion to Bahrain, $2.5 billion to Jordan, $830 million to Tunisia, and $1 billion to Iraq. While the focus here is on the UAE and Saudi Arabia, Kuwait is a frequent donor and provider of cash deposits, and Qatar provided ample support to Egypt between 2011 and 2013, made inroads to financially support Sudan and Somalia, and has made commitments (yet unfulfilled) to buy Lebanese debt in 2019 (American Enterprise Institute, 2021).

Sometimes, these promises remain just that—words. The advantage that commitments create can be as useful as actual delivery of support. But what is certain is that there is a shift in sources of direct financial support to emerging markets, as balance of payments support or cash deposits to central banks to shore up currency value, favorable loans, or extensions of credit through debt purchases. The shift is away from international financial institutions like the IMF and World Bank, and from US and European Union aid. The new masters of development finance are China and the Gulf Arab states. In the Middle East, Horn of Africa, and South Asia, these two forces are often working in synergy (Young, 2018b).

This trifecta of aid, investment, and direct financial intervention is a form of economic statecraft (Young, 2018b). Its rationale is the security and prosperity of the donor/investor. Because the Gulf Arab states have recognized a vital nexus between development and security in their surrounding geography, the logic of supporting friendly neighboring governments to secure political allies combined with investing for their own food security, real estate ventures, and state-linked energy projects is strategic. Their methods are often highly personalistic, and can create ripple effects and instability in domestic politics of the recipient state, especially in states in the midst of political transition. It can also be wasteful. When one relationship fails, or the recipient leader/interlocutor is out of power, the process begins again.

In the Middle East, the United States has arguably failed to provide a leadership role advocating in defense of liberal economic institutions and rule of law as a basis for economic development and political order since the beginning of the Arab uprisings in 2011 and in the eight years since. Not only is the perception of American disengagement becoming a reality on the ground in the Gulf, there is a real vacuum of financial resources and the ideals to stand behind them in transitions across the Arab world. Multilateral lenders and aid providers are simply outclassed and out-bargained. Whereas international financial institutions have used their leverage in providing access to finance to encourage prudent fiscal policy, transparency, and rule of law to support a liberal economic order, Gulf Arab aid, investment, and financial support has only one string attached: access (and not even loyalty).

But this is not an experience limited to the Middle East, or to tactics deployed only by Middle Eastern governments. The link to China's Belt and Road Initiative and the synergy between these states is accelerating the provision of finance to support energy production, petrochemical investment, ports and infrastructure investment, extractive mining, and industrial agriculture (Young, 2019). In short, the new development finance meets the shared needs of Chinese and Gulf Arab states, but has little concern for the needs of citizens in the sites of their intervention and investment.

Development aid and finance as we have known it since the Bretton Woods system formed is in a profound transition, with new actors, new sources of infrastructure finance, and new incentives for growth. In a recent panel discussion at the Brookings Institution, Alex Rondos, the EU special representative to the Horn of Africa gave an interesting analogy— "We provide nutrition; they give cocaine"—to describe how Gulf states and China offer a quick and easy fix to financial vulnerability (Brookings

Institution, 2019). This drugged finance is compared to official development assistance by traditional donors like the EU and United States. The problem is that the Bretton Woods institutions, the United States, and the European Union are in no position to compete with the amount of financial support or the speed of its delivery that the Gulf Arab states can offer. The best scenario is partnership and engagement, and a strong advocacy for institutional support, rather than head of state relationships.

2 THE GULF IN THE GLOBAL ECONOMY: GEARING UP FOR A POST-OIL ERA

Chapter Two is a study of the political economy of the Gulf in efforts to diversify from oil and gas rents, to monetize state hydrocarbon resources, and to start to reconfigure national oil companies into global energy powerhouses with conventional and renewable expertise. The chapter explains the synergy of Gulf-China relations both within the region and as these ties extend across high population and high growth economies to create markets for full-stream energy products, from petrol to petrochemicals and plastics, as a way to capture new markets and customers and form political alliances. For China, domestic labor markets and financial institutions have relied on outreach to developing economies. For the Gulf, outward investments and financial support have their own regime survival justifications. And while the current economic imperative is to find alternate sources of growth besides oil and gas, the key demands on the state to deliver services and opportunities for citizens remain the basis of the Gulf social contract model.

Delivering opportunity now means less direct employment from the state, but the state is still the facilitator of employment (even in the private sector) and the master planner of how and in which sectors the economy should grow. And while China has made its outward development assistance a center point of its foreign policy and South-South leadership appeal through support of multilateral development banks and regional organizations, the Gulf outward development approach tends to be more bilateral and less formal or publicly advertised, at least for now. The only Gulf

Cooperation Council (GCC) member state to actively expand its multilateral finance institutional membership and presence is the United Arab Emirates. This signals some divergence among GCC states in their approach to diplomatic and foreign economic policy engagement, and difference in how these states see their own role in a global development policy agenda.

The best way to understand how the Gulf states export a model of development is to start with their own history, and how these states provide a narrative of growth to their own citizens and residents. The forward-looking view of diversification, numerous development strategies and visions all reflect some key understandings and norms in the Gulf about the role and responsibility of the state to create economic opportunity and growth. And there are some very important distinctions between Gulf states and their leadership in early acceptance of the potential of resource wealth and how best to use it to improve the livelihoods of the region's people. Ideas about economic development and stateness, or the identity and capacity of the state in formation, are intertwined. These ideas have a past, and a basis in the construction of Gulf state identity.

Development States by Design

In Qatar, the UAE, and Oman, the battle for the development state includes inter-generational confrontation, with young leaders deposing their elders in order to accelerate a redistributive state-building project based on hydrocarbon wealth. In 1966, Sheikh Zayed deposed his half-brother in the Trucial States, later the UAE; and in 1970, Sultan Qaboos deposed his father in Oman. In Qatar, Sheikh Hamad overthrew his own father in 1995 to take charge of the exploitation of Qatar's gas reserves. In Saudi Arabia, equally confrontational (though with the blessing of his father, the king) has been the developmental state under Crown Prince Mohammed bin Salman (MBS) since 2016. MBS has staked his legacy on the state's ability to diversify and monetize its oil into dominance in other sectors, including renewable energy but also regional tourism, financial services, logistics, and transport. In each of these cases, it has been political leadership rather than market forces that is tasked and responsible for the economic development agenda. The ability to excel and grow despite the shifts in the global economy, including the volatility of hydrocarbon demand, is a kind of patrimonial obligation of the state to its citizens. Something good leaders know how to do. The more audacious the plan, the braver the leader.

These states have seen that natural resource wealth is a necessary but insufficient variable for economic growth. And while the myth of a wise and benevolent hereditary leadership is pervasive, there are also the examples of roads not taken. In the case of both Kuwait and Bahrain, their early discoveries and oil production brought wealth, institutionalization, and expanded new sectors of economic activity in these states. In the case of Bahrain, it introduced the concept of a financial services center to the Gulf. Bahrain was an early adopter of higher education opportunities for women and has generally had higher than regional averages of female workforce participation. However, oil resources are limited and the timing of entry to global energy markets is a large determinant of the trajectory of economic growth for these states. Bahrain began oil production in 1932 in partnership with Standard Oil and was in large part managed as a colonial protectorate of the British Empire from the 1800s until 1971 upon independence. Bahrain did not assume government control of the national oil company until 1980. Kuwait's oil production also began in the 1930s with significant exports by 1946. Kuwait won its independence from Great Britain earlier, in 1961, and its major period of industrialization and growth was between the 1950s to early 1980s. The height of the growth curve of these two states occurred earlier than that of their neighbors, and also during a period of relatively lower oil prices. For the UAE and Qatar in particular, their period of economic boom and expansion dovetails with historically very high oil prices, what I have called the "magic decade" of 2003–2014 (Young, 2020d).

But that early success in Bahrain and Kuwait has been followed by a kind of development stalemate. Two differences in the design of their political economies stand out. First, both Bahrain and Kuwait have monarchies with power diluted via parliaments and a long history of merchant elite families on similar socioeconomic footing to the ruling families. In Kuwait, a portion of oil revenues is specifically earmarked by parliament for savings to a future generation's sovereign fund. Second, their regional postures limit their ability to compete and challenge their neighbors directly. In the case of Bahrain, the shared oil field with Saudi Arabia and the relative size of the tiny island of Bahrain makes it nearly impossible to challenge the kingdom economically or politically. In Kuwait, the first Gulf war demonstrated the military vulnerability of Kuwait to the envy of its neighbors. Its foreign policy since the Iraqi invasion in 1990 has followed a neutral course. Domestically, business and investment tend to have an outward orientation, with less enthusiasm for domestic infrastructure and industry.

In some ways, the Gulf Arab monarchies are developmental states by initial design. The capacity for renewal is evident in the production of five-year economic plans and continuous "visions" of the future (Koch, 2017). That mandate is the social contract, and the continual need to demonstrate new plans and new ideas for growth has also created a wide berth for some of these states in their grandiose schemes of new islands, financial centers, logistics and transport hubs, and cities of the future. The learning that occurred in this state-building process has been a strong belief in the role of leadership, and a singular leadership rather than consultative or party-based politics in economic decision-making.

The second lesson has been a comfort with intra-regional competition and replication of national development agendas. No idea or project is off limits or proprietary. For example, even within the UAE, it has been common for Abu Dhabi to replicate economic innovations started in Dubai. The Dubai International Financial Center includes an arbitration court and legal code allowing businesses to enter contracts under UK or US law (Krishnan, 2018). Abu Dhabi Global Markets replicated that system and even hired many of the senior staff from the DIFC to start up its own financial center (ADGM, n.d.). The Gulf states regularly borrow and steal development practices and projects from each other.

The third lesson is a distrust of outside powers and a growing sense of establishing a name and place or positioning within global politics. Strategies of hedging between defense providers (and arms purchases from most of them), branding through sports teams and hosting international events and agencies, and omni-balancing (Gause, 2017). The outcome is that these states have become iterative developmental states, setting trajectories for themselves and re-evaluating on a regular basis. The positioning extends to great power relationships as well as intra-GCC power dynamics. The capacity for U-turns and abrupt shifts in alliances and adversarial positions is remarkable. Take for example the change in January 2021, as the Al Ula agreement formally ended the blockade of Qatar by the UAE, Saudi Arabia, Bahrain, and Egypt since July 2017. By September 2021, the emir of Qatar, the Saudi crown prince, and the national security advisory and brother of the crown prince of Abu Dhabi were posing for social media photo-ops in their swimming trunks together after nearly four years of bitter escalation to the threat of invasion and financial sabotage (Amwaj Media, 2021). The maneuverability in policy, whether in foreign policy or fiscal policy, is a privilege of centralized authority, but it is also a hallmark of Gulf policymaking across a number of issue areas. And as the Gulf states become more engaged and influential in the decision-making of other states, especially those that receive significant Gulf investment and aid, the expectation of malleability can be transferred.

The need to re-evaluate and reform economic policy, especially patterns of fiscal spending, usually relates to the volatility of oil prices. The yo-yo effect of belt-tightening when revenues are low and then expansionary fiscal policy when oil prices are high has long characterized the pro-cyclical nature of Gulf political economies. That had been the case until late 2014; the shale revolution has changed the immediacy of the diversification agenda and compelled the Gulf states to consider their future alliances and trade partners with new urgency.

Diversification for a Post-Oil Economy

The urgency of diversification has only intensified with the economic effects of the Covid-19 pandemic, into twin crises of plentiful supply of oil and a downward trend in the demand for oil. The context of the current economic reality of Gulf Arab oil exporting states begins in late 2014. Global oil markets are still contending with a fundamental recalibration of supply, which US shale continues to upend (Young, 2020b). The Organization of Petroleum Exporting Countries' (OPEC) response to the advent of shale production began with a partnership with non-OPEC members (mainly Russia and Mexico) in December 2016. That partnership has held, though it faced some volatile renegotiations in March and April of 2020 between Saudi Arabia and Russia, and then again in the summer of 2021 between the UAE and Saudi Arabia. Saudi Arabia has consistently defended market share, at the expense of low prices, in a bid to discourage shale production and to maintain key export contracts with buyers in Asia. 2020's oil price decline was especially expensive for the Saudi government, as government oil revenues dropped as much as 45 percent in the first half of the year. Tax revenue declined as much as 75 percent (Al Rajhi Capital, 2020). The duration of the Covid-19 impact on global oil demand is still unknown, even as lockdowns end in Asia and Europe, the return to global travel patterns, and work from home culture may spell an even steeper than expected decline in fuel demand.

Unfortunately, the global structural pressures of plentiful oil supply (much of it due to technological advances and efficiencies of US shale production), an expected plateau of oil demand from 2035 onwards, and the necessity of government stimulus to shield economic decline from the Covid-19 pandemic all make that shift more precarious (Dale & Fattouh, 2018). The recent reliance on foreign reserves and savings built up when oil prices were high in the "magic decade" between 2003 and 2014 is unlikely to be replaced in the near term, exposing the government to future fiscal vulnerability and possible currency devaluation. There is a revenue-to-expenditure gap across the GCC that will only widen without either a reduction in government spending or a significant increase in revenue.

Alternatively, in the short term governments must rely on debt to finance the deficit gap. Thanks to an external debt spree since 2015, the GCC states have made the Middle East a regional leader in bond issuance, ahead of Asia and Eastern Europe in emerging market external sovereign debt (Dehn, 2019). Gulf external sovereign debt issuance was negligible as a proportion of emerging market debt in 2008; by 2017 it was more than $50 billion in one year, and 2019 saw $52.9 billion in new government debt, outpacing chronic borrowers in Latin America. By the end of 2020, Gulf debt issues reached nearly $70 billion. While access to international debt capital markets has been good for all of the GCC states, including those with weaker credit ratings like Bahrain and Oman, governments are entering an addictive cycle, relying on debt to meet an annual funding gap. Saudi Arabia's government debt has ballooned from less than 100 billion SAR ($26.2 billion) in 2014 to more than 800 billion SAR ($213.2 billion) in mid-2020, with an increasing reliance on external dollar-denominated bonds (Al Rajhi Capital, 2020). The coming debt service burden will substantially restrict fiscal policy into the future. For Bahrain, gross funding needs are expected to reach 11.4 percent of GDP by 2024, meaning continued borrowing (Barclays, 2021).

GCC Economic Policy Response to the Twin Crises

The policy response to the twin crises is geared to meet two challenges, one short-term and one longer-term. First is the short-term challenge of domestic economic recovery and boosting domestic demand. Second is the longer-term fiscal challenge and the decisions necessary to reduce government expenditure. Fiscal belt-tightening is bound to focus on domestic expenditure in social services and public sector wages, but it will also need to come to grips with the foreign economic policy limitations of Gulf states' regional financial intervention, as a source of aid and investment across the Middle East, Pakistan, and the Horn of Africa (Young, 2020b).

Looking toward recovery across the GCC, we should expect these economies to continue to differentiate, but all will have a deepened reliance on debt-financing their deficits. They will be even more reliant on state-led growth, either as stimulus, or as a re-enforced pro-cyclical nature of their economies. As oil revenues stay low, we will see fewer government contracting awards, less economic activity, and pressure on local bank sectors to extend lending throughout the economy (Young, 2020a).

Most importantly, the twin crises of Covid-19 and low oil prices have been devastating to local demand in the GCC economies. For those economies that have smaller citizen populations as a proportion of total population, the threat of expatriate job losses, less disposable income and discretionary spending, and then repatriation or exit, all make the expected recovery more difficult. In those states with advances in the diversification agenda, the current global economic climate is not hospitable. What we have seen in non-oil growth is largely in sectors very sensitive to the Covid-19 pandemic: hospitality, tourism, travel (airlines), real estate, and logistics. None of these sectors fared well in 2020. And with government spending on contracts in decline, the obvious outcome has been job losses, but not just in construction and low-wage employment, but more across sectors and income levels—what some feared would be an expatriate exodus, which further dampens domestic demand (Nafie & Holtmeier, 2020). However, new policy initiatives to strengthen domestic demand by targeting high-income, well-educated foreigners as long-term residents has been one example of policy flexibility during the twin crises. Saudi Arabia, Oman (Elhamy, 2021), the United Arab Emirates, and Qatar (France24, 2020) all have new immigration policies to encourage property investors and skilled long-term residents, also a source of domestic demand for the retail and hospitality sectors (PwC, 2021).

From the International Monetary Fund perspective, the Covid-19 pandemic recovery has been very weak, with 2020 including a Middle

East regional negative GDP growth outlook, but especially downward in the oil producers, especially the GCC. The growth forecast was 7.1 percent for 2020 (IMF, 2020). The outlook across emerging markets was stratified. There was a stronger recovery and resilience in Asia, with much weaker recovery and outlook for Latin America, and then just slightly better across the Middle East and North Africa. From a sociological perspective, we are seeing recent gains in women's labor force participation under threat, as well as threats to a positive demographic dividend. The demographic dividend is the ability to capture a young and educated workforce to boost productivity. The exit from the pandemic and recovery from the 2014 oil price collapse could be a moment to harness the so-called "youth bulge," a population of young men and women who have had good access to education, health care, and only lack opportunity for employment, particularly in growing the private sector. To lose that momentum could be detrimental for years to come. As oil prices accelerated in late 2021, the allure of the pro-cyclical nature of reform loomed again, though this time most GCC states (all but Kuwait and Qatar) have instituted a value-added tax and restrictions to energy and water subsidies.

The scope of the pandemic stimulus across the GCC focused on suspension of fees, electricity fees in industrial zones, some discount lending to local banks, some deposits to local banks, a few small and medium-sized enterprise (SME) support funds, and direct transfer support to citizen workers in the private sector (notably in Bahrain, Kuwait, Qatar, and Saudi Arabia), but all were limited in terms of three to six months in 2020. At the same time, there is some movement toward austerity, including reducing the number of citizens receiving cash stipends for lower income families and raising value-added tax to 15 percent in Saudi Arabia. And in Oman, mandates of retirement for older citizens working in the public sector. Across the board, budget cuts to ministries in Oman and Saudi Arabia have been attempts to lower fiscal expenditure. Yet, at the same time, Saudi Arabia has vowed to continue some megaproject spending on projects that are unlikely to yield short-term job creation or private sector growth (England & Omran, 2020).

The future outlook, even with good access to debt capital markets, must include a period in which existing assets in foreign currency reserves and sovereign wealth funds are difficult to replenish without a substantial increase in oil revenues, with across the board break-even prices well above the $60/barrel range (mid to high $70s in Saudi Arabia, according to the IMF) for all of the GCC states. The period between 2003 and 2014 allowed a massive building of capital for Gulf exporters, and they can use those assets now. But even the Public Investment Fund in Saudi Arabia, which received a $40 billion transfer from the Saudi central bank, SAMA, in the first quarter of 2020, can allocate those funds to invest abroad, but there is no guarantee that they can amplify those investments at the rate at which the money was earned over the previous two decades (Sovereign Wealth Fund Institute, 2021).

Oil has been a great source of capital; it's not clear that a new growth strategy can equal that, or certainly work if placed abroad, or if invested at home, especially without foreign direct investment (FDI). And FDI has been weak, especially for Saudi Arabia in the last decade, and has not rebounded significantly, even with the efforts of Vision 2030 since 2016 (CEIC Data, 2020). And again, the diversification efforts across the Gulf have been highly sensitive to Covid-19, in tourism and entertainment especially, meaning that any recovery in FDI will depend on global markets for travel and tourism.

Across the oil exporters of the GCC, there is a persistent weakness in the private sector, especially in small and medium-sized businesses. For young people, this is a job creation issue, an issue of productivity increase, but it is also a symptom of a bank sector that is dominated by government deposits. For example, in Oman and Qatar 30 percent of deposits are government or government-related entities (GREs). There may be political pressure on local banks to help GREs, and as a result, the local bank sectors in the Gulf could find an increase in non-performing loans. Banks across the GCC are generally well-capitalized, but they are not necessarily well-positioned to help small and medium-sized businesses. There have been some efforts to create stimulus funds for SMEs in the UAE, Bahrain, Saudi Arabia, and Qatar; these are of disparate sizes relative to their economies, and generally a second-order stimulus compared to efforts to increase bank liquidity and ease lending restrictions. In Oman, instead of a direct fund to support SMEs, the government development bank granted repayment reprieves to borrowers.

The pressure to maintain social spending despite declining revenues is strong. The structural weaknesses are not due to Covid-19 or 2020; these are problems that have been evident since the oil price decline in late 2014, if not before. The simple math is that government spending and fiscal policy needs to be reined in. Saudi Arabia is trying to make major spending cuts on the one hand, while also holding on to megaprojects and finding it difficult to reduce defense spending in the Yemen conflict (Rashed et al., 2020). We could see more efforts, in Oman for example, to cut defense spending and the public sector wage bill. But the future of the region, in terms of social spending, benefits, and public sector job commitments, is ripe for a dramatic shift.

As for the regional consequences of the twin crises in the Gulf, the impact on remittance flows and employment for foreigners is stark. Governments in the Gulf Arab states have varied thinking on how best to retain talent and foreign workers, and how to use the current downturn to help "nationalize" their labor forces to include more citizens and fewer foreign workers. For the UAE, the necessity of domestic demand and consumption generated by foreigners makes immigration policy more flexible, at least to a certain income-level and skill-level.

For countries like Saudi Arabia and Oman, government sees the current crisis as a good time to shield and protect certain sectors and job categories for nationals only. Problematically, early evidence from Oman suggests that nationals are slow to take up positions vacated by foreigners, particularly in low-wage sectors (HSBC, 2021). Late 2020 and 2021 saw a decline in remittance flows from within the Middle East, as The World Bank (2020) suggested. This inequity combines with a real difference in the pace of recovery across emerging markets. Women stand to lose a great deal, especially those who are migrant workers in the GCC, as well as general female job losses for both low- and higher-wage earners, as the effects of the "She-cession" (Tannenbaum et al., 2020). Of many domestic workers across the Gulf, they are women who support families in the Philippines, in India, in East Africa, and these women are losing their jobs.

For Gulf Arab financial support in the form of investment and humanitarian aid, the outlook for future flows is somewhat uncertain. An increasing number of governments in the Middle East, Horn of Africa, and Pakistan look toward the GCC states as a source of foreign investment, and as a source of financial intervention, particularly to shore up support of their economies through central bank deposits and often oil and gas in-kind transfers. As the fiscal pressures of the twin crises are prolonged, these external obligations may shift in priority. At the very minimum, external financial commitments will become part of the national conversation on spending and shared resources between citizens and the state.

The twin crises of Covid-19 and the oil price decline of 2020 may be a turning point in the political economy of the Gulf Arab states, but the crises do not necessarily create easy policy options. The short term will likely be a shuffling through fueled by debt issuance, new taxes and fees, and a reliance on local bank sectors. Labor markets are certain to contract, but it is not yet clear that job creation for nationals will be an automatic benefit. For those states with smaller citizen populations relative to total population, the priority to stimulate domestic demand will translate to more open immigration policy, but with clear targets to higher-income consumers and potential investors. For other states, the fiscal deficits will require immediate budget constraints, increased tax and revenue schemes, and perhaps wider privatization efforts to attract foreign investment. Economic diversification measures reliant on tourism and hospitality will be subject to the global trends of a post-Covid recovery that remains elusive. Working from home cultural shifts and the timely dissemination of a successful vaccine may change local consumption patterns, but not necessarily travel and tourism demand. The outcome is a variation in policy response across the Gulf Arab oil exporters, and a possible recalibration of domestic demographics and labor markets.

And if nothing else, the trajectory of global economic recovery has been closely tied to the economic giant of China. The pandemic reinforced the sense that the economic health of the Gulf states is closely tied to that of its export markets in China and Asia more broadly. Problematically, that realization also came with a sense of escalating tension between the United States and China, with the Gulf Arab states very much caught in the middle. As Minister of State Anwar Gargash said in October 2021, "We're all worried, very much, about a looming Cold War," between China and the United States with the American security relationship under strain and the economic relationship to China more essential to diversification goals as well as continued energy exports (Fattah, 2021).

The Gulf-China Synergy

China's direct economic gains in the wider Middle East relied mostly on winning contracting awards from Gulf governments, including a recent award in Etihad rail in the UAE (Bhatia, 2020). As part of strategic partnerships, there is also equal interest from the Gulf side to become a part of the China One Belt One Road initiative. The appointment of Chinese contractors to Gulf infrastructure projects is a complementary Gulf state policy objective, as evidenced by the Dubai Silk Road strategy, which comprises nine initiatives and 33 projects aimed at enhancing the emirate's trade and logistics capacity (Oxford Business Group, n.d.).

After Saudi Crown Prince Mohamed bin Salman's state visit to China in 2019, investors signed memoranda of understanding worth $28 billion for projects in Saudi Arabia, including construction sector agreements with China State Construction Engineering Corporation (CSCEC); one such agreement was to build housing units (worth $667 million) for the Saudi National Housing Company (Yiu, 2019). CSCEC has completed $7.8 billion worth of projects in the Middle East in the last fifteen years and has $19 billion worth of contracts according to MEED Projects. In 2019, there were $520 billion worth of pre-execution phase projects in Saudi Arabia alone.

By 2021, Chinese solar firms had gained contract awards to help Saudi Arabia reach its ambitious solar electricity generation goals, in partnership with ACWA Power, a firm partly owned by the Saudi sovereign wealth fund, the Public Investment Fund (Aguinaldo, 2021). Outside of oil and gas, renewables have also been a focus of Chinese investment in the Gulf. In 2017, Abu Dhabi awarded a contract to a consortium led by Japan's Marubeni Corporation and China's Jinko Solar to develop a 1,177 MW PV solar independent power project at Sweihan, the world's largest single-site solar project (AP News, 2020).

China imported $6.7 billion (or 2.8 percent) of its total oil requirements from the UAE in 2018. But more than a key export market, China is increasingly an active investor in Gulf oil and gas infrastructure, including recent co-investments in Abu Dhabi National Oil Co (ADNOC) onshore concessions and new offshore concessions. In the summer of 2020, for the first time a dedicated Chinese offshore oil and gas company has joined ADNOC offshore concessions. PetroChina holds a 10 percent interest in the Lower Zakum concession as well as 10 percent of the Umm Shaif and Nasr concession. With the agreement, China National Offshore Oil Corporation (CNOOC) will hold 4 percent interest in Lower Zakum and Umm Shaif/Nasr, with PetroChina holding the remaining 6 percent (Saadi, 2020).

Total trade between the UAE and China totaled $50 billion in 2017, and 60 percent of Chinese goods imported into the UAE are re-exported to the Middle East and Africa, making the UAE more central to China's trade ambitions and networks regionally. Chinese financial institutions are also making inroads in the Gulf finance sector. The UAE's federal government-owned development bank (Emirates Development Bank-

EDB) issued its first bond in 2018 (after a decree allowing federal debt issuance), in which the $750 million five-year bond was arranged by Emirates NBD Capital, Industrial and Commercial Bank of China, and Standard Chartered. China's largest state-owned commercial banks— Industrial and Commercial Bank of China, China Construction Bank, Agricultural Bank of China, and Bank of China—have been increasing their market share in the Middle East. Also known as the "Big Four," these are the world's top four largest banks. With their first foothold established in the Dubai International Financial Center (DIFC), each of the Big Four has opened operating branches in the Middle East and North Africa (MENA) region since 2008. From their branches in the DIFC, these banks run major regional operations and continuously expand their activities. According to the 2015 full-year operating review results of the DIFC, Chinese banks in the DIFC doubled their balance sheet over a period of 18 months (Dubai International Finance Centre, 2016). As of March 2019, the Big Four contributed a quarter of DIFC's collective balance sheet for banking (Xueqing, 2019).

China is quickly becoming a major contender in large project development in the Middle East. Because Chinese contractors can often bid on awards with state-backed financing, they are able to assess and win projects with higher risks in new and less established markets. Chinese financing has played a significant role in a railway network in Iran and other projects in Iraq, Algeria, and Saudi Arabia, according to research by MEED in its "The Future of Middle East Energy" report (2018). These four countries, along with the UAE, accounted for 75 percent of the total estimated value of projects awarded to Chinese contractors in 2000–2017. China's total share of contracts awarded across the region was almost 13 percent, and Chinese contracting is expected to grow further. The UAE was a prime destination for Chinese policy lenders in the last two years, with $2.3 billion in loans, including financing toward the expansion of both Dubai International Airport and Al Maktoum Airport. Jordan came in second, with total lending valued at $1.7 billion, followed by Saudi Arabia with $977 million and Egypt with $890 million.

Looking towards new projects, Chinese firms are aggressively bidding on MENA infrastructure (Aguinaldo, 2018). They bid to build part of a railway in the UAE, a rail network already linked to Huawei technology products. MENA governments have encouraged Chinese firms to bid and often award contracts because they are the most price competitive, given their ability to rely on state banks for financing for projects that relate to the Belt and Road Initiative. The linkages of technology to infrastructure projects have created a sensitive collaborative model, in which companies like Siemens have agreed to partner with Chinese contractors in order to win participation in these large projects.

Competition and Transition: The Future of Gulf-China Economic Relations

Export-oriented growth now includes the provision of finance as service. The Chinese strategy of port development, large-scale construction services, and the provision of state-backed finance instruments is gaining traction in the Gulf, but it is also inspiring Gulf states to emulate this strategy, sometimes in the same places where China is engaged. As these forces combine, their incentives to create opportunity and development in recipient countries will differ sharply from traditional multilateral sources of development finance.

The synergy now created by both Chinese economic statecraft and Gulf states' increasing orientation eastward is a powerful force that will affect patterns of investment in emerging markets, but also practices of development finance, of post-conflict reconstruction, and ideas about appropriate governance of markets of the Middle East. Much of this relationship involves Gulf supply of China's seemingly insatiable demand for energy, but China is also eying the Gulf for its own industries and investment. China and Arab Gulf states are likely to use their capacities as financiers, contractors, and developers to increase ties and exert regional influence at a time when the United States signals a desire to be less engaged in the Middle East.

The future of growth for the Gulf states will rely on the control of ports and transit waterways (of the Red Sea corridor, Arabian Sea, and Indian Ocean), of export markets for energy products in Asia, and favorable access to the largest economies in the Middle East and Africa (Saudi Press Agency, 2018). Trends in urbanization and energy demand map closely to where the Arab Gulf states are now investing their political and economic resources (Reel, 2018). Chinese investment is symbiotic to Gulf security and economic objectives; though they are competing for many of the same projects, they are at times cooperative rivals.

China is a source of finance, a competitor in infrastructure projects, and a constant reminder of the power of alternative economic organization to the West. The growth in financial flows is compelling, but it requires constant feeding from its state-backed forces. Both China and the Gulf states use state-owned firms, including financial entities and banks, such that constant expansion of projects and financing serves a domestic objective on balance sheets as well (Teng et al., 2018). Some scholars term the expansion of Chinese state-backed lending as "debt book diplomacy" as the expansion serves a political goal of the Belt and Road Initiative, but also gives commercial purpose to a growing financial sector (Parker & Chefitz, 2018). Lending, however, is not as substantial as the gain from contracting awards and co-investments in the energy and transport sectors.

The opening of two new ports in Oman, Sohar and Duqm, along with the new Hamad port in Qatar, are adding shipping capacity and new mechanisms of regional integration, in spite of a difficult period within the Gulf Cooperation Council because of the tension between Qatar and its Gulf neighbors (Young, 2018c). China financed the development of the Duqm Port, as well as a new expansion of Khalifa Port in Abu Dhabi, and has an interest in their growth. Abu Dhabi's new Cosco Shipping Ports (CSP) container terminal at Khalifa Port serves to boost trade with China, but also competes directly with its sister port, Jebel Ali, in Dubai, which is currently the world's busiest port outside of Asia. Khalifa is set to be the largest container freight station in the Middle East, the result of a 35-year agreement between Abu Dhabi Ports and Cosco Shipping Ports Ltd, a subsidiary of Cosco Shipping Corporation Limited of China (Rahman, 2018). The port agreement comes on the heels of President Xi Jinping's 2018 official three-day visit to the United Arab Emirates, the first by a Chinese leader to the Emirates in nearly thirty years. The UAE is China's second-largest trading partner and its largest export/re-export market within the MENA region. In addition to their "Comprehensive Strategic Partnership," the UAE and China have gone beyond shared investment and trade ties to increasing cooperation on security and counterterrorism issues (Fulton, 2018).

China clearly articulated its policy toward the Arab world and its economic interests in its 2016 Arab Policy Paper, which detailed its interests in trade agreements and technology (Government of China, 2016). Energy supply is a key, but not exclusive, concern; increasing bilateral trade and tourism from China to the Arab world is also a policy objective. The value of commercial activity between China and the GCC states accelerated from just under $10 billion in 2000 to nearly $115 billion in 2016 (Qian & Fulton, 2018).

This growth in bilateral trade flows continues and by 2018, according to research by First Abu Dhabi Bank, the GCC states now account for China's largest source of oil and the second largest provider of its gas needs (Saidi, 2018). China is likely to become the GCC's largest export market within the next two years (Menon, 2014). The increase in trade ties is not one way; by 2020, GCC imports from China were expected to double in value to around $135 billion. Flows of people are increasing as well, as a recent estimate showed a 40 percent increase in Chinese tourist arrivals between 2014 and 2017 (Forest, 2018).

Both Saudi Arabia and the UAE are courting Chinese investment in shared energy projects, encompassing traditional oil production and renewable capacity and energy storage. State-owned enterprises Aramco and SABIC aim to partner with China's Sinopec and China North Industries Corp, creating a synergy of government firms. In the UAE, these projects include a contract worth $1.6 billion between ADNOC and the China National Petroleum Corporation (following an earlier $1.17 billion investment in Abu Dhabi's offshore fields) (*Gulf News*, 2018). In addition, there is a partnership and investment agreement between Dubai's Electricity and Water Authority (DEWA) and China's Silk Road Fund to create the world's largest solar energy plant (Arabian Business, 2018). In November 2018, ADNOC signed a new agreement for the sale of liquified petroleum gas (LPG) to Wanhua Chemical Group of China, owner of the world's largest underground LPG storage facility (Bridge, 2018). According to research by Qamar Energy, there are at least ten current energy projects planned or active in the GCC with Chinese investment, from traditional and solar electricity generation, to pipeline development in the UAE, methanol production in Oman, and uranium exploration in Saudi Arabia (Mills et al., 2017).

The recent growth in ties is based in China's demand for energy and the Gulf's ability to provide an important and growing market. China requires energy, especially to supply its infrastructure and construction boom as it builds new cities. Automobile sales in China quadrupled between 2008 and 2016, and transportation needs have also increased petroleum and related product demand. As China seeks to shift its own energy mix away from polluting coal-fired power plants, its demand for gas has multiplied. The most important factor driving global gas consumption in 2017 was the surge in Chinese gas demand, where consumption increased by over 15 percent, accounting for nearly a third of the global increase in gas consumption (BP plc, 2018). It may create some leverage for Gulf major gas producers to shift China's attention their way in the first phase of a post-oil transition, as liquified natural gas is considered a bridge fuel to more renewable sources.

The Gulf states are competing with each other to secure China as an export market for their energy products beyond just oil and gas. The proliferation of downstream energy products in petrochemicals, including the construction of new refineries and chemical plants, is both a diversification strategy and a new product arena (and profit maker) for Gulf state energy companies (Paola, 2018). Despite this synergy of interests, there is already conflict, as evidenced in the recent dispute over control of shares of the Doraleh Container Terminal in Djibouti between DP World, the Dubai-based port management company, and the Djibouti Ports Authority (PDSA). Djibouti forced DP World out of the site by nationalizing the terminal; notably, the government partner of the port authority, the Hong Kong-listed China Merchants Port Holdings Company Ltd, a company overseen by Beijing's State Assets Supervision and Administration Commission, holds a 23.5 percent ownership stake in the terminal (Mooney, 2018). Effectively, the government of Djibouti made a choice of prioritizing ties to China as an investor, over its commercial ties to DP World.

Yet, there is a demographic dilemma in China, and it will acutely affect the oil exporters of the Gulf. It poses the most serious threat to the political economy of the region, and that includes the legitimacy of ruling families. A report from the investment bank Natixis finds that population aging in China will be fast and furious, with a steep decline on economic growth rates, from 6 percent a year in 2010 to 2.5 percent by 2030, with real impacts on global potential growth (Cheng, 2021). Chinese imports currently account for 12 percent of global imports. Today, Chinese consumption of global commodities (as a percent of global consumption) is about 15 percent of global oil and about 8 percent of global gas. As domestic demand falls with an aging population that is not replenished, that commodity demand will fall. Saudi Arabia may still pump the last barrel of oil, but it will most certainly also be the cheapest barrel and one that fewer consumers in China will need.

Perhaps the competition that China provides to the United States is best described as security at the fringes. As Afshin Molavi (2020) describes, China's ability to provide technology products that the United States does not offer the Gulf Arab states has been a wedge into Gulf markets and a wedge between the GCC states and their traditional security provider in the US. From the sale of drones to providing 5G technology, China's niche provisions do not compare to the level of US military sales or military training exercises shared in the Gulf Arab states. But the fact that China has become more needed as a source of technology, especially for defense, is an increasing source of tension with the United States.

But the idea of a forced choice between superpowers, in a Cold War scenario between China and the United States, is not realistic for the Middle East. There are states that are more vulnerable in their need for access to finance, for which China might be a valid alternative. And there are states that are simply serving their export markets and seeking longer-term investment partners. And there are states that have few other options. The problem in pitting the US versus China in each of these situations is ignoring a larger universe of investment sources and partners, whether private, multilateral, or state-supported in nature. The GCC states themselves are equally, if not more, important as China in the Middle East as sources of capital investment and job creation, not to mention less formal sources of aid and bilateral government support.

When it comes to foreign direct investment, aid, capital expenditure, and job creation, China is often characterized as the investor of choice in the Middle East. It is often erroneously labeled as the region's most important source of FDI. Certainly, China is a major source of FDI in a few places, especially in the GCC. When Chinese investment does arrive, it usually targets the energy sector and large government contracts. China's investment can be volatile, with surges and then declines; in fact, globally, China's 2019 outgoing investment was the weakest since 2011 (Young, 2020a).

When compared with American and European private investment efforts, China spends less and creates fewer jobs in most of the Middle East, North Africa, and West Asia (Islamic Development Bank, 2018). Indeed, the GCC states have higher capital expenditure and create more employment across the Middle East and North Africa than China—and that's not counting remittance flows, aid, financial intervention such as central-bank deposits, and in-kind oil and gas transfers (Young, 2018b). China is active as a regional investor and contractor where private capital doesn't want to go—places like Iran, Syria, and, to a degree, Turkey. One notable exception is the United Arab Emirates, where Chinese investment and contracts have surged since 2016 (Sahloul, 2020). This skews the data and inflates China's reputation as a regional investor and source of capital. The view that China is the largest investor in the Arab region overlooks the fact that Beijing has invested inconsistently over time, and picks and chooses its engagement in the broader region, from Morocco to Pakistan. The assertion also fails to mention that the GCC is a major source of FDI in that same geography, and also in the Horn of Africa.

China and the Gulf are linked and will continue to rely on each other for trade, investment, and partnerships in the years ahead. But these partnerships are in no way cemented on any ideological basis or security pact. The numerous strategic partnership agreements, and their various levels of engagement, demonstrate the limits and diversity of intention of China's reach in the Middle East, as Jonathan Fulton (2019) describes. And as the energy exporters of the Gulf seek to diversify their own economies and become more engaged in the production and expertise of renewable energy, China could become less of a customer and less of an active local investor. This insecurity in the Chinese commitment to the Gulf has led some states to diversify their own economic partnerships and to think more expansively about regional and international diplomatic and institutional engagements.

The Gulf States in Multilateral Finance

Another mechanism of development outreach is via bilateral and multilateral development finance institutions. China has entered this space with vigor and is now the world's largest source of bilateral development finance (Ray et al., 2021). Sovereign lending is a key feature of the Belt and Road Initiative. China's use of its own development banks, the China Development Bank (CDB) and the Export-Import Bank of China (ExIm Bank), accounted for more committed sovereign finance than the World Bank from 2009 to 2018 in Latin America and the Caribbean, and for five years in that decade, the two of them provided more sovereign finance in Africa than the World Bank (China Africa Research Initiative, n.d.; Gallagher & Myers, 2022).

The global landscape of development finance institutions (DFIs) includes multilateral DFIs, the private sector arms of international financial institutions (IFIs), which have been established by more than one country and are subject to international law. Shareholders in multilateral DFIs are usually national governments, but may also include other international or private entities. Multilateral DFIs provide finance to projects in the private sector usually through equity investments, long-term loans, and the provision of guarantees, essentially securing the debt that private lenders may also contribute to a project. Traditionally, multilateral DFIs have been able to amplify or provide more financing than bilateral DFIs, but that is no longer always the case, as we see with the provisions made by Chinese bilateral DFIs. Major multilateral DFIs include: the African Development Bank (AFDB), the Asian Development Bank (ADB), the European Bank for Reconstruction and Development (EBRD), the Inter-American Development Bank (IDB), the International Finance Corporation (IFC), and the Islamic Development Bank (ISDB).

Bilateral DFIs are independent institutions that generally receive discretionary seed funding from their governments to deploy on the basis of a return on the investment. Some major OECD country bilateral DFIs include: the OeEB (Austria), BIO (Belgium), BMI-SBI (Belgium), FinDev Canada (Canada), IFU (Denmark), Finnfund (Finland), AFD/Proparco (France), KfW/DEG (Germany), CDP/SIMEST (Italy), FMO (Netherlands), Norfund (Norway), SOFID (Portgual), and COFIDES (Spain). In the United States, the Development International Finance Corporation (DFC) replaced the Overseas Private Investment Corporation (OPIC) in January 2020, with a larger capacity to lend (Saldinger, 2020).

Until very recently, really after the Arab uprisings of 2011, the preference among Arab countries and Arab development finance institutions has been bilateral concessional finance and direct aid. Reporting has also been less transparent historically. But for Arab countries and institutions that share reporting to the OECD, between 2013 and 2017, concessional development finance from these government-backed banks totaled, on average, $12.6 billion per year (OPEC, n.d.). The United Arab Emirates and Saudi Arabia were the most significant bilateral providers of development assistance. And in 2017, according to the OECD, the UAE had the highest official development assistance/gross national income (ODA/GNI) ratio (1.03 percent) of all countries sharing reporting data to the OECD. Egypt and Yemen were the largest destinations of Arab state development bank concessional finance.

Recently, in 2021, the United Arab Emirates applied and succeeded in joining the EBRD as a shareholder. The EBRD has a mission to support financing in governments with a democratic commitment, yet it does not hold the same standard for its shareholder members as contributors to the bank's lending pool (Chadwick, 2021).

There are some interesting parallels in the shift in China's participation and reliance upon bilateral development finance institutions to more membership, leadership, and participation in multilateral development banks (MDBs). These are strategies of economic statecraft, to use membership and inclusion within member state institutions to build a network of sovereign clients, and also to establish a framing and practice of development finance. China has created a template for literally changing the structure of development finance to suit its own foreign and domestic policy needs. The Gulf states, too, have taken notice.

Scholars, including Humphrey and Chen, working on China's lending practices to developing countries describe the influence on the kinds of development projects that China tends to support, which tilts lending practices within institutions (Humphrey & Chen, 2021). Chin and Gallagher term this a "coordinated credit space," meaning the use of both bilateral and multilateral finance for Chinese banks and state-linked firms to fund and do contracting projects abroad, the "going out" of Chinese foreign economic policy (Chin & Gallagher, 2019). The Belt and Road Initiative has been a vehicle and mapping of this strategy, but the pace and amount of Chinese lending has ebbed, with highs in the early 2010s and then after 2017 bilateral lending largely plateaued. The other aspect of the bilateral lending has been its "hidden" quality (Horn et al., 2019). Borrowers and lenders do not necessarily report the debt in their dealings with international financial institutions (Tan, 2019).

China's practices in the last twenty years in development finance have legitimized more bilateral lending and quiet financial support, often for state infrastructure projects with very visible and political effects. The movement has widened the role for developing countries to expand their ties to each other, but also to expand their roles within existing multilateral institutions. Chinese political ideology—and government strategy— openly discusses the connection between China's deserved place as a global power, but also its positionality as a developing country. Such that China is able to access lending from institutions in which it is a shareholder like the World Bank, International Monetary Fund, and Asian Development Bank. The state identity as a developing country allows China some policy leniency on international trade agreements and now also climate change policy.

At the same time, China avoids association with "oppositional" Western institutions linked to wealthy nations, like membership in the OECD or Paris Club of lenders. China's 2021 White Paper on International Development explicitly describes a national aspiration in development partnership, shared economic goals in developing countries with China, and national economic strategies that are independent (State Council of the People's Republic of China, 2021). In many ways, the Chinese strategy is to avoid a global consensus on development practice, aid, or mechanisms of transfer and institutional accountability. It privileges economic ties that are "hidden" and a bilateral agenda. But at the same time, China's public amplification of its role in international institutions is one of global leadership.

China has created co-financing funds in large MDBs, built relationships with a number of smaller MDBs around the world, and established two new MDBs in which it has a central administrative and governing role: the Asian Infrastructure Investment Bank (AIIB) and the New Development Bank (NDB), formerly called the BRICs bank. The AIIB is larger in its membership, with close to 100 member states, including five of the largest national economies in the world. Bahrain, Oman, Qatar, the United Arab Emirates, and Saudi Arabia are AIIB member states; Kuwait is not (Asian Infrastructure Investment Bank, n.d.). Of the Gulf states that are members of the AIIB, Saudi Arabia has the largest share of voting rights with about 2.5 percent, while China holds about 26 percent of voting shares. But the NDB is a development bank led by only developing nations, by design.

For the Gulf states, the pattern that China has established as a facilitator of development finance, a founder and contributing member to a number of finance institutions at both the bilateral and multilateral level, legitimates a model of financial intervention that melds cache of institutional leadership with the profit-motive of state-related contracting firms, connected lending of the local bank sector, and deployment of co-investment funds that require no lengthy disclosure or prospectus. The UAE is following this pattern as well, with the exception that it is far less likely to also be a client of these banks in the way that China is both a lender and borrower. For both states, deposits and investments in multilateral development banks also provide a mechanism of a return on investment for capital, but also a political return on investment in the decision-making of allocations to client governments. The UAE, and other Gulf Arab states, have repeatedly used the strategy of co-investment funds via their sovereign wealth funds to partner with energy market competitors like Russia. The strategy is not the same as membership in a multilateral development bank but using state-owned investment funds in partnership with very little reporting or transparency in their capital allocations or return on investment success.

It is also clear that there is increasing demand from developing countries for more financial intervention, particularly investment and lending for infrastructure projects. The 2015 Addis Ababa Action Agreement (AAAA) is one example of an international agreement and effort to form a consensus on how best to meet the finance needs of growing countries (Office of the United Nations High Commissioner for Human Rights, n.d.). The third international conference on finance for development under the auspices of the United Nations reached some essential agreement on the demand for infrastructure investment, but also welcomed the addition of new multilateral and regional fora to provide access to loans and credit. The agreement calls for a global infrastructure forum, building upon and working with multinational finance institutions and names the AIIB and NDB as particularly welcome. In specifics, the agreement notes a global infrastructure investment gap, which amounts to $1–1.5 trillion annually within developing countries. And while this strong demand for investment has been met with new initiatives led by China, the Gulf states also find themselves with an opportunity to engage. The NDB has just five core members: Russia, Brazil, China, India, and South Africa. Bangladesh joined in September 2021. But the prospective members under consideration are very interesting (and quite different): the United Arab Emirates and Uruguay (New Development Bank, n.d.). Uruguay does not have the fiscal capacity to be a major shareholder and lender within the bank; rather it can exist under Brazil's umbrella, tagging onto lending efforts and regional development initiatives. For the UAE, however, there is capacity to become a shareholder on par with the original members. Moreover, the UAE has the capacity to deploy contracting and delivery of infrastructure projects in borrowing countries.

While the UAE stands out among its GCC peers for its diplomatic and multilateral engagement on development finance issues, the regional commitment to increasing the stature and lending capacity of Arab development banks is somewhat diminished. The Islamic Development Bank (IsDB), for example, has 57 member states including all six of the GCC states. Saudi Arabia is the largest shareholder with just over 23 percent of capital contributions, with the next highest contribution at about 7 percent from the UAE, among the Gulf states. The bank lends globally, not just in the Middle East or Muslim world, but at a limited scale. Its niche in recent South-South development efforts has been the issuance of "green" sukuks, or Islamic bonds, which meet both Islamic legal requirements and the environmental, social, and governance (ESG) objectives of a growing set of investor preferences (Islamic Development Bank, 2021a). The bank has set a goal of 35 percent of its operations to be in climate finance by 2025.

The longer tradition of pan-Arab development funds dates to 1961 with the creation of the Kuwait Fund for Development. This model of transferring oil wealth within a pan-Arab identity set of recipient states and using concessional finance mechanism has been the norm among resource-rich Gulf states. Yet, this model did little to advance a method of economic development or ideas about state-led growth, and was more to do with a forward payment and access to concessional capital based on an identity affiliation and ideological transfer of wealth for the Arab world. As Nidal Sabri outlines, these funds operate within an Official Development Assistance (ODA) framework in which the lending is at a discount to commercial rates, at favorable repayment and negotiable terms including a grant element, and often center on certain kinds of sectors (transportation and energy, predominantly) (Sabri, 2008). Most of the lending practices take equity positions in projects (rather than interest payments), as a mechanism consistent with Islamic finance. Some funds have fared better than others, emblematic of the volatility of oil wealth in their own national economies. Thirteen development funds fall into this category:

1 Arab Monetary Fund
2 Arab Fund for Economic and Social Development
3 Arab Bank for Economic Development in Africa (BADEA)
4 Inter-Arab Investment Guarantee Corporation
5 Arab Gulf Program for United Nations Development Organizations (AGFUND)
6 Arab Trade Financing Program
7 Islamic Development Bank
8 OPEC Special Fund for International Development

9 Abu Dhabi Fund for Arab Economic Development

10 Kuwaiti Fund for Arab Economic Development

11 Saudi Fund for Development

12 Iraq Fund for External Development

13 Libyan Arab Foreign Investment Company

In some ways, the experience of the Arab development funds mirrors (and pre-dates) the Chinese "going-out" strategy, at least in the provision of finance to a wider sphere of influence with the benefit of cycling out domestic investment for a return earned in a third country. But these funds have not been as successful in promoting national contracting firms or industry in the way that Chinese foreign lending and development institutional linkages have. Nor did they come with the added benefit of job creation or entrepreneurship advances for nationals in the ways that the Chinese "going out" strategy has done, especially in Africa. Most importantly, these efforts are largely bilateral and have rarely worked in partnership with larger multilateral financial institutions or United Nations development agendas. (One exception is the Islamic Development Bank, which has been more concentrated in following the UN sustainable development goals and a shared South-South agenda.)

The Gulf Arab state development finance model is therefore uniquely linked to the volatility and pro-cyclical nature of oil revenue. Gulf politics and foreign economic policy, whether through aid or development finance, has also had its ebbs and flows, starting with the 1960s interest in pan-Arab identity and development, and morphing more to direct intervention and support by the 2011 Arab Spring. The institutionalization of development finance has also been somewhat stagnant, with a few notable exceptions. In the next chapter, in the case of Egypt, we see an effort to bridge support using the International Monetary Fund as a partner. And this chapter has demonstrated the outlier case of the UAE as a burgeoning member of more multilateral development finance entities, like the EBRD and the NDB. This is a departure from regional practice and either demonstrates a self-confidence in the UAE's own diversification model to be exported, or a combination effort to enhance diplomatic standing and international organization membership to differentiate itself within the region and brandish an identity on a more global (rather than pan-Arab) scale.

3 BEST CASE SCENARIOS? CASE STUDIES OF GULF FINANCIAL INTERVENTION IN EGYPT AND ETHIOPIA

The cases of Gulf financial intervention in Egypt and Ethiopia demonstrate the capacity of competing forms of financial support to achieve foreign policy goals. Egypt's receipt of aid and investment flows from Qatar between 2011 and 2013, and then the UAE and Saudi Arabia from 2013 to 2020 illustrate this trend, in its political nature and also in the deep capacity Gulf states have for financial intervention. More than $80 billion went to Egypt from the Gulf in the form of central bank deposits, foreign direct investment, and state-sponsored support in this decade, 2011–2020. The coordination of multilateral support, in Egypt's debt package from the International Monetary Fund is also novel in this period, as it entailed Gulf commitments of support.

In Ethiopia, we see the extensive use of sovereign wealth funds to allocate foreign direct investment as a political commitment of the UAE, and to a lesser degree of Saudi Arabia. The chapter explains why Ethiopia is a target of interest, and how these commitments were often difficult to uphold, given the structural barriers of Ethiopia's financial system and its regulatory hurdles (a closed banking system), and a difficult domestic political transition under Prime Minister Abiy Ahmed.

Despite the political challenges in both of these countries, Egypt and Ethiopia represent an economic opportunity and test environments for a future energy market growth thesis. These two cases also exemplify the "best case scenario" of developing economies as recipient targets of aid and financial intervention, especially increased access to capital for infrastructure investments. The demographics are poised for accelerated growth. Population growth in Africa is the most dynamic demographic story in emerging markets today, according to research by HSBC (van der Linde & Pomeroy, 2021). With population growth stagnating or declining in most of the world, African population growth is projected to reach 4 billion by the end of the century, nearly matching Asia. African labor supply, productive capacity, and local consumption will all expand significantly. Trends in urbanization, smaller families, and women's workforce participation will shift consumption patterns. Africa might also become a site of labor-intensive manufacturing in competition with Asia as income and wage growth there accelerates. The ability to "leapfrog" industries through digitalization could create growth opportunities in financial services, online retail shopping, and mobile communications. There will also be a growing demand for electricity and energy products more broadly in transport and logistics.

To capture that growth opportunity now, there is an opening for strategic partnerships and large-scale investment generally through government rather than private sector channels. The Gulf states, especially the UAE, Qatar, and Saudi Arabia, have been willing to enter a space and at times compete with China as a source of capital and in addition, a source of direct political support. For the Gulf states, the chokepoints of the Suez Canal, and along East Africa and the Horn are most compelling as sites of financial intervention, as they match with strategic throughways of energy exports as well as new military and port facilities. For these reasons, this sub-region in Africa has become a site of strategic competition among the Gulf states.

Oil Booms, Aid, and Financial Intervention

The Arab Gulf states, or the member states of the Gulf Cooperation Council, or GCC (Bahrain, Kuwait, Oman, Qatar, Saudi Arabia, and the United Arab Emirates), have historically used foreign aid and humanitarian aid as a quiet tool of their respective foreign policies within the wider Middle East. More recently, however, we have seen targeted financial aid and military assistance by these states, particularly Saudi Arabia, Qatar, and the UAE, towards neighbors in crisis since 2011. The UAE, Saudi Arabia, and Qatar have used financial and military aid to jockey for influence within Egypt's evolving political leadership, to attempt to remove Syria's Assad from power, to counter the growth of the Islamic State movement in Iraq, to influence political battles in Libya, and in democratic Tunisia. Windfalls in wealth generated from the rapid ascent of oil and gas prices between 2003 and 2014 allowed budgets to expand for both military expenditure and financial aid. The dramatic fall in oil prices in late 2014 raised questions about the ability of these states to continue their generosity and the exercise of economic statecraft in the MENA region. The shift that occurred really after 2016 was not necessarily a diminished use of tools of economic statecraft, but more of a focus on returns on investment and since 2021, less of an interest in direct confrontation with Gulf neighbors.

Theoretically, we might ask how the movement of oil prices correlates with Gulf financial aid and more interventionist foreign policy historically since the 1970s. One might expect Gulf aid to be dependent on the ability of states to earn income from natural resources; the price of carbon energy should have some effect on aid allocations. However, historically the flow of Gulf aid at least has not always correlated with oil prices. So, while there is a shift from more traditional forms of aid and assistance to a more developmental, interventionist, and investment-driven approach from the Gulf states after the Arab Spring, there is also a continuation of a very strategic priority of financial aid and intervention, which is not always hyper-sensitive to the price of oil and the state of fiscal coffers. Strategies are what has changed, from quiet aid and support to more forceful intervention with both financial and defensive levers, to a more investment-minded approach by 2021.

Strategies among the Gulf Arab states have evolved, but so too has the development assistance ecosystem. This is a factor of emerging South-South connectivity, but also the tilt toward economic growth and political engagement away from Western donors. Historically, the Development Assistance Committee, or DAC, formed in the 1960s to coordinate and promote aid from donor states of the Organization for Economic Cooperation and Development. The DAC is a community of shared values, in that its members largely problematize development as appropriate relationships between state and market in the liberal democratic tradition (Kragelund, 2008). Gulf Arab states are not "emerging," but rather diverging from the DAC norm, as their targets of aid and their practice of giving differ from the pro-capitalist, pro-democracy conditional aid from prominent Western donors. Nor are the Gulf states new donors; rather, the Gulf Arab states have been active donors in waves since the discovery of oil and state foundation in the 1960s and 1970s. The largest donors of the sub-region have been Saudi Arabia, Kuwait, and the United Arab Emirates. Since the 2000s, Qatar has increased the amount and visibility of its aid.

Windfalls in wealth generated from the rapid ascent of oil and gas prices between 2003 and 2014 allowed budgets to expand for military expenditure and financial aid. While the dramatic fall in oil prices from late 2014 (falling from a year peak of $107 per barrel in June 2014 to a low of $50 per barrel in January 2015) certainly impacted the ability of these states to continue their generosity and the exercise of economic statecraft in the MENA region, the short-term aid decision-making suggests a different logic. Fiscal policy pressure and foreign policy objectives have recalibrated aid and financial intervention, but not necessarily led to abrupt stops.

Both oil resources and foreign aid are "sovereign rents," so there should be some commonality in the experiences of states that earn these rents and use them to facilitate an economic development agenda (Collier, 2006). There is also the argument that the Gulf states prefer some recipients over others on cultural and religious bases of support, and there is certainly a tradition of financial support among the Islamic Ummah or global community (Neumayer, 2003). The Gulf Arab states, particularly since 2011, have relied on a number of aid mechanisms, including non-restricted cash grants, injections to central banks, and in-kind oil and gas deliveries; the investment drive comes a bit later, after 2016 perhaps as a reaction to the shift in oil markets after the US shale revolution, but also as a learning curve of aid injected after the Arab Spring.

Oil Price and Gulf Arab Foreign Aid: Not Always Closely Linked

There is a positive correlation between the price of oil and Gulf Arab state aid, but it is not always so closely linked. There are episodes in which oil prices rise without a respective increase in Gulf foreign aid. There are also very recent examples of the Gulf states extending tremendous development aid at a moment in which oil prices are at historical lows and the fiscal budgets of the Gulf states themselves are facing deficits. The politics of Gulf Arab state aid is, above all else, strategic. Political goals can override economic prudence. The reverberation of this shift challenges both norms and foundational institutions of North-South interactions (Acharya, 2004). At an investor conference in Sharm al Sheikh in March 2015 (at which Egypt received new offers of Gulf aid), the Egyptian minister of investment, Ashaf Salman acknowledged receipt of at least $23 billion in combined direct funds from Saudi Arabia, Kuwait, and the UAE since General Sisi came to power in late summer 2013 (Georgy & Kahlin, 2015; Shenker, 2015). The Egyptian case between 2011 and 2016 is an example of financial support in very large tranches, with little strings attached (see Table 3.1).

The use of oil and gas products as aid in-kind, the targeting of construction and real estate as both investment vehicles (for state and private sector firms) and employment strategies, and the manipulation of foreign reserves and central banks as quick fixes to a depreciating currency, all of these strategies relate to Gulf practices in economic governance. The Gulf Arab states regularly use the availability of oil and gas products, at steeply subsidized prices, to stimulate otherwise inefficient manufacturing and construction industries, while at the consumer level, provide a cost-of-living rebate. There is a kind of replication in economic governance via aid that we can trace specifically in this period in Gulf aid to Egypt.

Gulf economies are highly concentrated in provisions of investment vehicles, mostly in construction and real estate because these sectors facilitate *Sharia* compliant investment, while they also work in line with government spending cycles (Arvai et al., 2014). Most of the GCC states have restricted monetary policies tied in some form to the US dollar. They are not experienced with extreme currency volatility (or hyperinflation). It may be that donor expectations are that a hard currency deposit in a central bank should stabilize an economy. The cash deposits could in fact exacerbate the inflation problem, as monetary policy becomes reliant on the external source of hard currency to maintain a target exchange rate. There is evidence that aid volatility and windfalls, particularly in cash deposits, create incentives for receiving governments to increase consumption and fiscal spending (Kharas & Desai, 2020, pp. 5–6). This, in turn, creates volatility in the exchange rate (inflation), which is also linked to lower growth.

TABLE 3.1 *(Select) Gulf Arab state aid to Egypt: 2011–2015*

Country	2011	2012	2013	2014	2015
UAE	$3bn (of which $1.5bn Khalifa bin Zayed fund for housing and small and medium-sized enterprise support) **Private reported aid: $22.8m**	**Private reported aid: $22.19m**	A grant of $1bn and a further $2bn deposit with Central Bank of Egypt. In-kind (petroleum and gas) $225m		4$bn aid package: $2bn to Central Bank of Egypt, and $2bn project finance
Saudi Arabia (KSA)			A total of $5bn aid package: $1bn cash grant, $2bn in-kind (petroleum and gas), $2bn deposit with Central Bank of Egypt		$1bn pledge to Central Bank of Egypt ($3bn investment pledge)
Qatar	$500m cash grant; $2bn deposit with Central Bank of Egypt	$1bn cash grant; approximately $4bn deposit with Central Bank of Egypt			
Kuwait			$1bn cash grant; $2bn deposit with Central Bank of Egypt		$4bn investment pledge

Sources: UAE Ministry of Foreign Affairs, African Development Bank Group, KSA Ministry of Foreign Affairs, Qatar Ministry of Foreign Affairs.

Historically, the Gulf Arab states have increased aid for political goals related to shifts in the international political economy. After the 1973 oil embargo, petrodollars rapidly accumulated in international banks, creating the lending boom to developing countries. OPEC surpluses in 1974–1976 were close to $142 billion, while developing country deficits reached around $80 billion (Momani & Ennis, 2013). Gulf Arab foreign aid was an average of 12.48 per cent of gross national product (GNP) at the height of the oil boom in 1973 (Nonneman, 1988, p. 133). Andre Simmons has argued that Gulf aid was targeted to developing countries (through multilateral and bilateral institutions) to lessen the sting of post-embargo wealth among developing economy peers (Simmons, 1981). During the 1980s through the 1990s, Gulf Arab state donors exercised more restraint as oil revenues decreased, on average 2.38 per cent of GNP by 1985 (Nonneman, 1988).

After the Iraqi invasion of Kuwait in 1991, the Gulf Arab states prioritized security over development aid and a more interventionist or public display of foreign policy goals. There was a brief spike in Gulf aid in the reconstruction effort in Kuwait, which quickly diminished by the mid-1990s (Barakat & Zyck, 2010, p. 9). As Momani and Ennis demonstrate, Gulf Arab foreign assistance reduced by half in the late 1990s ($1.3 billion) compared to 1990–1994 ($2.6 billion), in itself a period of restraint (Momani & Ennis, 2013). The period following the second Gulf war and American invasion of Iraq in 2003 had a profound effect on Gulf Arab state donor practices. Under intense scrutiny by Western governments for their support of Taliban Afghanistan before 2001, the Gulf states recalibrated aid targets and, in some cases, made more efforts to present their aid practices as global poverty reduction programs (Cooper & Momani, 2009). The Dubai Cares model, created by Sheikh Mohammed bin Rashid (ruler of Dubai), is a case in point, in which donors shifted from traditional Arab or Muslim country recipients to those globally in most need.

The second oil boom of 2003–2008 created an aid dilemma for the Gulf Arab states, in that the largesse of the early 1970s was not to be repeated, either because state priorities (and constituent demands) for domestic spending had increased, or because the states saw little reward in the exercise of aid to gain prominence in international institutions or to acquire allies in other developing states. GCC official reserves increased from $53.5 billion in 2003 to $514.3 billion in 2008, yet foreign aid increased only modestly, back to levels of the late 1980s (IMF, 2008).

Momani and Ennis (2013) estimate Gulf Arab foreign aid between 1985 and 1990 as $3.1 billion.

The figures below track Gulf Arab state aid from the 1970s to the present, using official development assistance (ODA) data from the OECD. The data itself is politicized, as we have a limited view of official government aid from Gulf Arab donors, while private donations (often sourced from members of the respective ruling families of Gulf monarchies) go unreported (Shushan, 2011). The Gulf Arab states have made efforts to streamline reporting of official aid since the first decade of the 2000s. The UAE made its first foreign aid report in 2013 and has since created an institutional framework to track and coordinate state aid efforts (UAE Ministry of Foreign Affairs & International Cooperation, 2021). Kuwait has perhaps the most long-standing transparent aid framework of the Gulf Arab states, at least in its channeling of aid through one institution, the Kuwait Fund for Development. Private donations in Kuwait continue to be a source of concern to many Western governments. Qatar has also begun to report their foreign aid and to attempt to track private charity within the sheikhdom (Tok et al., 2014). Saudi Arabia makes the least effort to publicly account for its donor activity, though (like the UAE and Kuwait) it has managed a formal institution, or fund, for state directed development aid. Villanger stresses the historical Emirati, Saudi, and Kuwaiti preference for bilateral aid via funds, rather than via multilaterals (OPEC fund, IMF, Arab Monetary Fund, etc.) contributing to the divergence in norms between Gulf Arab aid and OECD Development Assistance Committee (DAC) donors (Villanger, 2007). There is also significant divergence among Gulf Arab donors, particularly after 2001 in their aid practices, donation amounts, and in their reporting of aid. Figures 3.1, 3.2, and 3.3 illustrate these differences.

Theoretical and Practical Implications of Gulf Arab Foreign Aid

Foreign aid is clearly a priority of Gulf Arab state foreign policy. However, foreign aid's track record for efficacy, at least in the comparative experience of Western donors to developing countries, is questionable. The literature and empirical evidence, both in qualitative studies and large-N surveys, reveals foreign aid is no panacea. Like a resource curse, aid can act as an exogenous shock to developing political economies, entrenching

FIGURE 3.1 Saudi Arabia (KSA) official development aid and oil prices, 1970–2013. *Sources*: ODA from OECD.stat and Brent crude prices from BP Statistical Review of World Energy 2014.

FIGURE 3.2 Kuwait official development aid and oil prices, 1970–2013. *Sources*: ODA from OECD.stat and Brent crude prices from BP Review of World Energy 2014.

problems in governance and financial volatility, even as it seeks to alleviate human suffering (Tirone & Savun, 2012). Governments seeking to promote strategic goals have had little success in also creating incentives for liberal economic reform agendas in aid destinations (Bearce & Tirone, 2010). Aid creates allies, or it might propel reform and economic growth, but not usually at the same time (Burnside & Dollar, 2000).

Scholars know that foreign aid can extend the tenure of inept and corrupt rulers and governments (Ahmed, 2012). In fact, work by Faisal Ahmed demonstrates that sources of resource rents (including remittances and foreign aid) can prolong a government's rule if used to

FIGURE 3.3 United Arab Emirates official development aid and oil prices, 1970–2013. *Sources*: ODA from OECD.stat and Brent crude prices from BP Review of World Energy 2014.

reward elites, even while worsening aggregate welfare (2012, p. 161). Gulf states are also balancing demands for domestic spending, including welfare benefits and infrastructure investment, at moments of incremental public concern for fiscal deficits and lower oil revenue. The Gulf Arab states are engaging in a long debate on the efficacy of aid with their own set of norms and priorities, which are not necessarily cohesive within the sub-region. Most of the critiques of foreign aid concentrate on the problem of governance and how aid does little to change the behavior of corrupt or inefficient regimes (Easterly, 2008).

And while the post-Arab Spring period might have provided an opportunity for the Gulf Arab states to create foreign aid projects with new approaches to job creation and public-private partnerships, what transpired was a recalibration from using tools based in aid, to tools based on investment and to mutual benefit, rather than no-strings giving. The UAE investment in Egypt and efforts to build a new capital city is one interesting example (Parasie, 2015). Qatar's investment in food security in sub-Saharan Africa is another (Bailey & Willoughby, 2013).

Gulf Arab state aid, though enabled by resource wealth, is not historically tied directly to the volatility of these commodity prices, at least up to 2015 and the start of the current energy transition. The impact of the shale revolution and fall of oil prices in late 2014 begins a period of profound fiscal adjustment and diversification in the Gulf states. It also begins a period of reckoning with the longer-term outlook for hydrocarbon resource revenue generation. Global oil demand is expected to peak sometime around 2030, and the momentum of global policy restrictions around carbon emissions is likely to change the way the Gulf states direct investment into their own economies, as well as the way that they see the benefit of aid and investment into the regions around them. Recipient states that may be good consumer markets for electricity or renewable energy products, as well as traditional hydrocarbons including petrochemicals, may be favored sites of intervention.

Egypt's Centrality in Gulf Foreign Policy and Intervention Efforts

In 2011, Egypt landed at the ideological center of a dispute between Qatar and its fellow GCC members Saudi Arabia, the United Arab Emirates, and Bahrain. The battle over support for Islamist political movements and intentions to support political activism in neighboring states continues to weigh heavily in the Gulf even as the resolution achieved with the Al Ula agreement in January 2021 restored diplomatic ties and transit links. In the decade between 2011 and 2021, Egypt became ground zero for experimentation of the Gulf states in foreign policy interventions via deployment of economic statecraft (Young, 2017a). Egypt has also emerged as a test case of economic reform in the wider Middle East and North Africa in the post-Arab Spring environment.

While Qatar supported the Muslim Brotherhood candidate and then President Mohamed Morsi in post-revolution elections in 2012, by July 2013 he lost power to the counter-revolution led by military leader turned politician General Abdel Fatah al-Sisi. Qatari financial support for the Morsi government included loans, investment pledges as well as direct support. The UAE and Saudi Arabia were adamantly opposed to the Morsi government and quickly mounted a counter-support effort for al-Sisi in 2013. As Cochrane (2021) argues, there was a noted shift for the UAE in 2013 in its official development assistance (ODA) contributions, with the ODA increasing by nearly 600 percent year on year. After 2013, Emirati ODA declined each year to 2020. The UAE government has linked its significant increase of foreign aid in 2013 to fulfilling its commitment to the Millennium Development Goals (UAE Ministry of International Cooperation and Development, 2013). Yet the increase in overall ODA in 2013 from the UAE is equal to its direct support to Egypt, rather than spread among a wide set of recipient case countries.

In efforts to shore up Egypt's political stability since 2013, the UAE and Saudi Arabia used a number of financial tools, including: deposits into the Egyptian Central Bank, favorable loans, in-kind donations of oil and gas shipments, and promises of foreign direct investment in sectors like real estate and agriculture (Young, 2016b). There was considerable volatility in the flow of Gulf financial support to Egypt between 2013 and 2016, as the steep decline in oil prices in late 2014 shifted Gulf fiscal priorities and the impact of support in Egypt may not have met donor or investor expectations (Young, 2016b). An optimistic Egypt Economic Development Conference (EEDC) in Sharm el-Sheikh in March 2015 elicited offers of aid and investment from Kuwait, Oman, Saudi Arabia, and the UAE of more than $12.5 billion (Georgy & Kahlin, 2015). But by the next year, Egypt also returned to seeking assistance from traditional multilateral finance sources including the World Bank and International Monetary Fund to meet its fiscal crisis and stabilize its currency (Associated Press in Cairo, 2016).

The UAE and Saudi Arabia concentrated much of their support flows to Egypt in foreign direct investments from state-related entities, particularly in real estate (Egypt State Information Service, 2017). A sticking point of Gulf economic statecraft, particularly from the UAE, is its preference for beneficial investment opportunity to the state and its related commercial entities, often funded by investment vehicles made up of the private resources of public figures (Halligan, 2014). Foreign aid and investment are not charity, even when their target is a primary foreign policy priority.

Egypt's geographic and political positioning is useful to the Gulf but also precarious in the deployment of aid and investment, as its economic interests remain divided between factions within the GCC. While it is no longer indebted to Qatar for loans extended after 2011 (having made repayments in 2014 and 2016), outstanding debt payments to other Gulf states continued to weigh on its spending commitments (Reuters, 2016).

Egypt's relationship with Qatar is also complicated by their mutual reliance on liquefied natural gas (LNG) exports and transit. Even though Egypt has its own LNG industry, it is a purchaser of Qatari LNG. Egypt's own ability to meet its energy needs has been volatile, as its gas production and export capacity decreased sharply in 2014, causing a crisis in domestic power production. In 2013, natural gas accounted for 51.5 percent of the total primary energy supplied in Egypt and produced 76.8 percent of its electricity capacity (Meighan, 2016). New exploration contracts halted after the uprisings of 2011 and 2013, even as demand for electricity production continued to expand from Egypt's growing population. Again in 2021, Egypt suspended LNG exports as it sought to reconfigure how to meet external export commitments, including possible export to Lebanon, along with meeting its own domestic gas needs (Stevenson, 2021). According to Platts Analytics, Qatar exported 78.8 million metric tonnes (mt) of LNG in 2016, more than 30 percent of a total global supply of 257.8 million mt, with an increasing share of its production delivered to Egypt, Jordan, and the UAE (Energy Egypt, 2017). During the blockade of Qatar by the Saudi, Emirati, Bahraini, and Egyptian quartet from June 2017 to January 2021, Egypt never blocked exports of Qatari gas through the Suez Canal, but it did bar Qatari vessels from stopping along the way in Egypt's ports and its economic zones (Arab News, 2017).

Egypt might also be regarded as a test case of some of the economic reform measures the Gulf states began to implement at home, though the GCC states are generally better positioned to pick and choose among necessary structural reforms from subsidy reductions to implementing taxes. Egypt has implemented a full-on structural adjustment, attempting to tame a fiscal deficit, an inflation problem, an external debt burden, high cost subsidies, a poor tax infrastructure, and a reliance on foreign direct investment and tourism (its main source of foreign currency earnings) (Reuters, 2017a). Egypt is a kind of bellwether for the Arab world especially after 2011 for the ways in which society reacts to economic reform (especially subsidy reductions), something that Gulf governments and rulers are very careful to observe for reflection in their own societies.

Scholars examining the effects of energy subsidies in the Middle East and North Africa find that the opportunity cost of directing government spending toward energy consumption (in the form of subsidies) has negative effects in inefficient industries and starving out of other government portfolios like health and education, which make better longer-term investments of state funds (Bassam & El-Katiri, 2017). In the wake of the Covid-19 pandemic, there is reason to further study how the trade-offs in investments in public health over other social spending affects economic recovery. And how might injections of financial support better strengthen areas of the private sector and the provision of public goods? Like Gulf citizens, but with much more severe domestic consequences, Egyptians face high unemployment and obstacles to economic inclusion, especially for women. From 2013–2016, investment in Egypt's political stability and economic growth was a core foreign policy priority of the UAE and Saudi Arabia; after 2016, we see a slow disengagement, or at least a more concerted effort to replace aid and direct financial support with more targeted investments with expected returns.

The Evidence of Financial Intervention in Egypt

From the Gulf Financial Aid and Direct Investment Tracker at the American Enterprise Institute, we compiled data on foreign direct investment flows from both state-related and private entities from the six GCC states to Egypt from 2003–2021. In addition to this, we combined reported official development assistance, along with cash transfers in the form of central bank deposits and commitments of in-kind oil and gas transfers. This section outlines some of those findings and also compares the foreign direct investment flows from the Gulf with those from China, the United States, the United Kingdom, and the European Union.

Several findings emerge from this data collection. The first key finding is related to job creation as a result of financial intervention and investment. Over a two-decade period, from 2003–2021, the GCC states are the source of the most job creation in Egypt when compared to investment flows from China, the US, UK, or EU (Figure 3.4). For China,

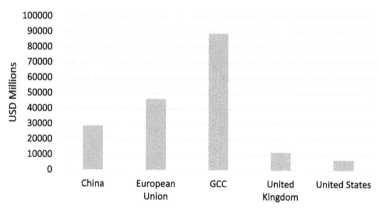

FIGURE 3.4 Capital investment in Egypt. *Sources*: American Enterprise Institute, fDi Markets.

which is a strong investor in Egypt, the comparative weak level of job creation is particularly instructive. Total jobs are also a weak indicator of total economic development impact, as the level of construction labor and lower wage opportunities likely outweighs those of higher-income and productivity jobs.

A second finding is that the amount of foreign direct investment flows from the GCC to Egypt in the period between 2003 and 2021 outweigh those of other key investors and regional blocks (Figure 3.5). By looking at foreign direct investment flows, we see a picture of global market sentiment toward Egypt. In the case of Gulf and Chinese investment flows, we also must account for state-owned investments directed at political ends. But at the same time, there is reason to see moments of political openness and opportunity that private investment flows gravitate toward as well. Figure 3.6 gives a more detailed picture of the pace and swings of capital investment into Egypt in moments of geopolitical and regional turmoil. The Arab uprisings in 2011, the sharp fall in oil prices in 2014, and the Covid-19 pandemic might expect dips in investment, except from the Gulf states the opposite occurs.

We also see interesting moments of surges. For China's investment flows into Egypt, this is particularly marked between 2015 and 2017. Foreign direct investment (FDI) flows from China in 2016 alone account for more than half of the total in the period from 2003–2021. China's reputation as a core investor in MENA is often misrepresented, as the investment tends to be in one-off large projects and inconsistent over

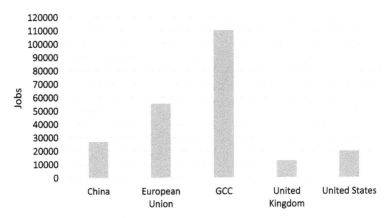

FIGURE 3.5 Job creation in Egypt. *Sources*: American Enterprise Institute, fDi Markets.

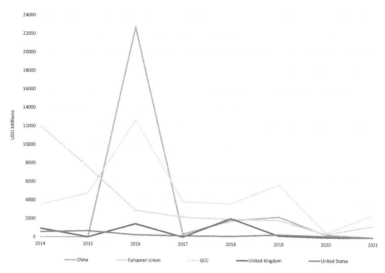

FIGURE 3.6 Capital investment in Egypt, 2014–2020. *Sources*: American Enterprise Institute, fDi Markets.

time. Chinese FDI into Egypt is also less of a job creator than other sources, especially those more consistent in their investment over time.

GCC capital investment in Egypt over the period 2003–2021 is larger and more consistent over time than from other peer investor states and regions. The FDI trend line in Egypt has been subject to political volatility and the intra-GCC investment trend is part of that story, but when compared to the entry and exit from other regional peer investors, the Gulf has provided a firm link within the MENA regional investment sphere.

When we look at volatility related to economic crises, from the Global Financial Crisis in 2008–2009, the sharp drop in oil prices in late 2014, to the Covid-19 pandemic in 2020, there is also an impact on Egypt, as was the case in most emerging market economies in their efforts at attracting FDI.

Yet, in each of these instances of crisis, the GCC has been the source of a surge of investment to Egypt. And in the case of the late 2014 oil price decline, we also see an instance in which investment from the United Kingdom increases briefly. Egypt's economy and sources of external support improved after 2014, in large part due to financing from the IMF and a commitment to structural economic reforms by the Al Sisi government. Even in the period in which China is most active as a source

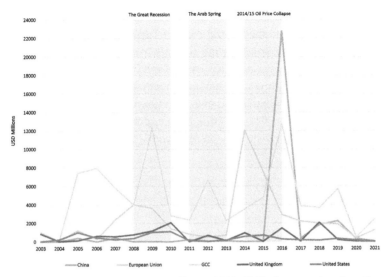

FIGURE 3.7 Capital investment in Egypt, 2003–2020. *Sources*: American Enterprise Institute, fDi Markets.

of FDI in Egypt in 2016, the GCC states combined offer more, and offer more in terms of job creation, as highlighted in the period from 2014–2020. And what is not included as foreign direct investment, but is probably equally if not more important from the Gulf, is remittance flows. Egypt's incoming remittances amounted to $31.4 billion in the fiscal year 2020–2021, the largest on record, and a source of domestic capital injection that far surpasses its foreign direct investment scale. Egypt attracted less than $6 billion in FDI in 2020, for example (Reuters, 2021c).

The start of the stabilization program in 2016 led to an improvement in investor confidence. Egypt used that improvement to expand its external borrowing, and the increase in external sovereign debt rose at one of the highest paces globally, doubling to $137 billion by the second quarter of 2021. Egypt's external debt to GDP level is still lower than many emerging market economies, but this period of rising debt also mirrors a similar trajectory by the GCC states in the period between 2016 and 2021. The reliance on debt issuance in the GCC to meet fiscal spending priorities sharply increased after the 2014 oil price downturn. The difference in the Gulf debt spree versus that of Egypt is that five years after the initial economic structural reforms began, the Gulf states (except the weaker ones like Bahrain and Oman) can continue to access debt capital markets with less reliance on investor sentiment on capital inflows.

In the fiscal year 2020–2021, Egypt also repaid a $2 billion deposit from Saudi Arabia to the Central Bank of Egypt Central. This increases the pressure on the government's reserves to both meet the needs of domestic banks' foreign currency demand and the government's external debt repayment resources. The mounting repayment schedule for coming debt maturities is demanding. Long-term external public debt will total $56 billion between 2021 and 2025, including $9.8 billion in Eurobonds (or foreign currency denominated debt) and $11.3 billion in repayments

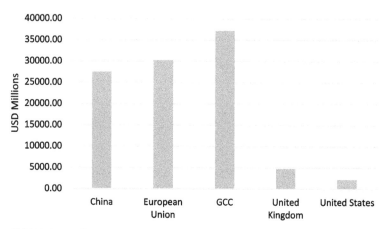

FIGURE 3.8 Foreign direct investment in Egypt, 2014–2020. *Sources*: American Enterprise Institute, fDi Markets.

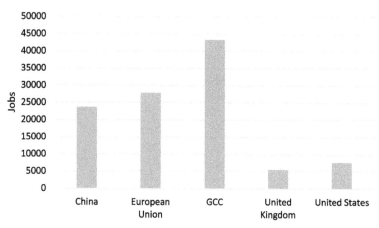

FIGURE 3.9 Jobs created in Egypt, 2014–2020. *Sources*: American Enterprise Institute, fDi Markets.

of loans due to the International Monetary Fund. The support in central bank deposits from the GCC states, namely Saudi Arabia, the United Arab Emirates and Kuwait, which flowed after 2013, is unlikely to repeat, pushing Egypt toward a new IMF package or a severe limitation of government resources to service debt above new spending pressures.

When we look at the investment side of Gulf financial support to Egypt, there are a number of key sectors and actors that emerge as integral to that support. First, there is divergence among GCC states in their ability and choice to support Egypt and how their investment outflows to Egypt shifted in the period from 2003–2021. In Figure 3.10, we see that there are considerable differences in the timing and amount of investment flows from the GCC region over time into Egypt. In moments of crisis, particularly in the global financial crisis, Arab Spring, and oil price collapse, support has varied. Qatar's investment flows to Egypt are strongest between 2008 and 2010, and then between 2011 and 2013. Interestingly, we can attribute the flows during the global financial crisis less to a political motivation and more to opportunity seeking and after 2011 as more political in nature. When we break down the firms engaged in investment in Egypt from Qatar in both periods, we find that there are just two large investments that account for these spikes.

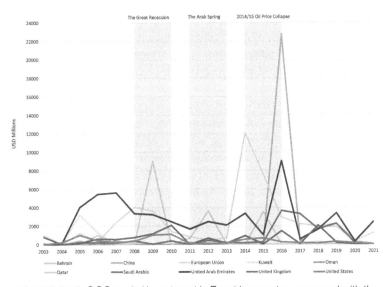

FIGURE 3.10 GCC capital investment in Egypt by country, compared with the US, China, and EU, 2003–2020 *Sources*: American Enterprise Institute, fDi Markets.

Over the period of 2006–2013, capital investment from Qatar to Egypt consisted of just nine major investments over $2 million. Three investments topped $1 billion. The first was an investment by Barwa Real Estate of $1 billion in 2006, followed by a massive $9 billion investment by the same firm in August 2009. This transaction alone accounts for the surge we see in the financial crisis period. Barwa Real Estate is a Qatar-based real estate company, whose business activities include the brokerage, sale, purchase, management, operation, refurbishing, and trading of land for construction in accordance with Islamic Sharia principles. The company is also involved in construction material production, banking and investment, as well as real estate and fund portfolio management activities. The company operates through a number of subsidiaries and joint ventures locally and internationally. Barwa Real Estate Company is headquartered in Doha. The company is Qatar's largest listed property developer and is owned partially (with a 45 percent share) by the Qatari Diar, the property arm of the sovereign wealth fund, a government entity (Reuters, 2012).

The 2009 investment by Barwa in Egypt was part of the new capital city residential housing initiative (Reuters, 2009). The 2012 Qatari flows to Egypt are mainly one investment by Qatar Petroleum International, also a state-owned entity and a subsidiary of Qatar Petroleum. This project was a $3.6 billion investment in the oil and gas sector. Qatar Petroleum International develops and produces ethylene and the company also developed an oil refinery in Panama. In both cases, we see a Gulf state-owned entity making an investment or allocation with high impact in a moment of otherwise low FDI from other regular or more consistent sources.

After 2013, the Qatari investment flows cease and we see a surge of investment from the UAE and Saudi Arabia. Even Bahrain signed a memorandum of understanding with the Egyptian Electricity Holding Company (EEHC), the state-owned operator, to create a Build-Own-Operate-Transfer solar power plant along with a consortium of investors in this period (Kiganda, 2020). The Bahraini capital investment in 2015 is a private investment from Terra-Sola, which is a solar investor and developer which committed to build a $3.5 billion solar electricity project in Egypt, though in 2021 this project was not yet off the ground. The company is a Swiss-German company with a base in Bahrain, but as of 2021 operates more from an Egypt office and a home office in Switzerland.

Capital investment originating in the United Arab Emirates was perhaps more consistent from the early 2000s to 2020, with a clear spike or increase in 2016, probably the high-water mark of UAE support to Egypt from public and private sources. One of the most important sources of investment from the UAE into Egypt between 2013 and 2018 was the real estate development arm of the Majid al Futtaim group, a private Dubai-based real estate and retail conglomerate. Other core investors include DP World and a series of traditional energy firms, like Dana Gas, to renewable firms like Alcazar and Access Infra Africa. One of the largest commitments of real estate investment from the UAE into Egypt was from Arabtec, with a $40 billion project in the new capital city announced in 2014 (Arnold, 2014). By 2020, the company (publicly listed on the Dubai exchange, but with a major state-owned shareholder Mubadala) filed for insolvency (Barbuscia & Al Sayegh, 2020). The contracting model of the Gulf in which state spending feeds a lucrative contract cycle in construction suffered a series of setbacks after the oil price decline of late 2014, with some ripple effects outside of the Gulf as well.

One of those places in which we see the effects of the procyclicality of Gulf state spending and investment that relays into contracting and overlaps with state-sanctioned political support is in Ethiopia.

Aid vs. Investment in the Age of Shifting Oil Demand

The twenty-first century is certainly the age of the Global South, as new actors emerge as key drivers of growth, and as South-South ties more distinctly shape how global energy markets move. The wealth of the Gulf states since the 1960s has been a reservoir for humanitarian assistance especially within the Arab and Muslim world, but the oil price boom or magic decade between 2003 and 2014 did not necessarily correlate directly to increased humanitarian assistance from the Gulf, as described earlier in this book.

But something else has occurred, and even been reinforced since late 2014 when the shale oil revolution pointed to the direction of volatility ahead, the new age in which our global economy moves more toward low or zero carbon energy sources and the plentiful nature of oil resources helps drive down price. Aid or official development assistance from the Gulf is now disproportionately originating in the UAE. GCC ODA flows to emerging markets accounted for about 20 percent of total official donor disbursements during the 1970s oil shocks, but then declined significantly during the 1990s. With the rebound in oil prices, the aid proportion from the Gulf did not bounce back. Official development assistance (reported to the OECD) from the six GCC states from 1974 to 1982 was consistently in the range of $15 to $20 billion per year. Between 1992 and 2002, that dropped to less than $2 billion. Saudi Arabia was the most important source of Gulf ODA from 1970 to about 2010. Since 2010, the UAE has emerged as the GCC state with the largest group contributions yet the overall contributions from the Gulf have never rebounded to their 1970s giving (based on 2019 dollar amounts). However, it was 2015 before GCC combined ODA reached $15 billion again and has since averaged under $10 billion per year between 2015 and 2021, led by the UAE (Razgallah, 2021).

There is also a general distinction between Gulf aid to the Middle East and North Africa and that to sub-Saharan Africa. The Middle East is the primary destination of Gulf aid, accounting for 40 percent of total disbursements to the region in 2019. Africa comes second as a major destination of Gulf aid, concentrated in Egypt, Morocco, and East Africa (Ethiopia and Sudan). Sudan is a stand-out case, with a major inflow of aid in 2019 of $312 million (to be discussed in a later chapter), along with Eritrea and Somalia. Somalia received its highest aid donation of $102 million in 2016, the same time that DP World won a concession to develop and operate a port in Berbera, Somaliland. So while the total amount of Gulf aid has diminished in comparison to the largesse of the 1970s, there is a shift to more targeted aid and more limited country sources within the GCC. The Middle East as a whole receives significant attention, and especially areas of conflict like Yemen have seen major inflows from Saudi Arabia and the UAE since 2015. But the growing importance of East Africa and the Horn is a novelty of Gulf financial aid and intervention that is truly a factor of a shift in energy markets and a shift in Gulf aid and investment strategy since 2014.

The Horn as a Strategic Location in the Gulf Lens

The expansion of a Gulf sphere of influence into the Horn of Africa accelerated after 2015, but many of its roots are in the Arab Spring after 2011, with a strong desire especially from the United Arab Emirates to seek to shape a security and economic zone around it. The first target was

Islamist politics. The second target may have been Iran. Opportunistically, Saudi Arabia and the UAE saw a moment to counter Iranian influence in the Horn through Sudan and Eritrea, as both of these governments opened to more of a partnership with the Gulf Arab states. Eritrea had granted Iran access to its Assab port in 2008, which by 2015 became a worrying prospect for Saudi Arabia and the UAE as the Houthi assault on the Yemeni capital in Sanaa previewed the possibility of more Iranian influence and potential transfer of weapons from the Red Sea into Houthi possession (Cannon & Rossiter, 2018). This is the same port which Ethiopia controlled until 1993 when Eritrea broke away and gained independence. Ethiopia had access to Assab until 1997, but then relied mostly on the port of Djibouti. It was Ethiopia's trade volume through Djibouti after 1997 that necessitated the expansion of that port and started the domino effect that led DP World to engage there as an operator before paving the way for larger commercial and military vessels in the port, then eventually the local government was convinced to renege its operation agreement with DP World and to give an operating concession to a Chinese entity. All of these changes have been in the last twenty years or so, a period of intense competition both within the region and among external actors. The Gulf states have stepped into a regional strategic competitive theater. The rationale for intervention was clear, and the willingness of politicians in the Horn to engage the Gulf states also seemed to have accelerated after 2015.

Of course, there are also long-standing ties in the flow of people from the Horn to the Gulf, many through Yemen to Saudi Arabia, and the consistent reliance on agriculture imports from the Horn. For the Gulf states, the security consideration from the Horn is about stability, pushing back the growth of Islamist political organizations, food supply chains, and also a forward-looking view of new markets for Gulf investment and energy products. What is certain is that the view of regional security from the Arab Gulf states is increasingly broadening in scope, as is the toolkit they use to confront their security challenges. From the use of aid, investment, military training, and operational presence in the Horn, there is an active engagement to achieve foreign policy goals.

In the Horn, multiple port concessions and security partnerships have occurred in iteration, often after preceding attempts produced disappointing results. Early patterns of economic statecraft demonstrated an emphasis on achieving value for money, while more recent attempts have prioritized state security concerns overachieving economic returns, especially as the war in Yemen has elevated the security component to a major policy priority since 2015 (Young, 2017a). At this stage, the UAE's evolving foreign policy in the Horn has produced mixed results on the commercial and economic fronts, some important wins on the peace and security fronts, and exacerbated some of the volatility in the region.

The exercise of economic statecraft is not an invention of the Gulf Arab states, however, and all states will use the tools at their disposal to create influence and opportunity, and to minimize threats to their security. Interventions with financial tools, and even incentives to private sector investors, do not always yield intended results. There have been disappointments and reactions to this policy trajectory, as the UAE has found with large housing projects in Egypt and its port concession in Djibouti, which the local government reverted to Chinese control. There is a foreign policy learning curve underway. Early indications suggest that the UAE in particular has a tendency to exit quickly, extract investment and aid commitments, and re-double efforts in new locations and with new partners. This shift could be seen as creating redundancies, and certainly a low concern for the efficiency of public investment and resources deployed.

Ethiopia's Swift Rise, and Risk to Fall

Ethiopia may struggle to secure port access to the Red Sea, but its economic potential does not seem to have been stunted since the loss of the Eritrean territory and port access. Access to infrastructure investment, including the Ethiopia-Djibouti electric railway built and financed by China, is one prime result of the Eritrea split and the momentum of Ethiopia's domestic economic acceleration, beginning in 2011 as a memorandum of understanding and culminating in the opening of the 750km railway by 2016 (Global Infrastructure Hub, 2020). In fact, Ethiopia's rise as a regional power seemed somewhat unstoppable, at least until 2021 and the outbreak of new hostilities among its rival political and ethnic factions, including a government crackdown led by Prime Minister Abiy Ahmed (Paravicini et al., 2021). Ethiopia's large population of 100 million people, its strong and well-equipped military, and its good natural resources of water and land make it enviable to neighbors. The timing of the Abiy administration beginning in 2018, the interest of the

BRI project outreach, and the availability and intersection of Gulf finance have all coincided to propel Ethiopia's economic boom. Whether it can continue will be more of a result of its domestic leadership.

Yet, there is the question whether the intersection of external actors with authoritarian capital, set some preconditions for the centralization of authority and tendencies toward the use of violence that in 2021 Prime Minister Abiy adopts. Chinese investment and Gulf investment in Ethiopia have surged, but there has also been a sharp increase in US based capital investment into Ethiopia since 2018. In fact, 2018 saw a massive inflow of external support and debt restructuring as Ethiopia secured $1 billion in an IMF support package in 2018, $3 billion in loans from the World Bank, $100 from France's Agency for Development, and renegotiated $4 billion of its debt to China, extending the repayment period by twenty years (Seleshie, 2021). Ethiopia has more than $12 billion in outstanding debt to Chinese state banks (Maasho, 2018).

How has that capital been put to work in the domestic economy and what institutional reform or stagnation might it support? The data below display some of those capital flows and the pull-out discussion of individual firms and foreign state-entity financed projects gives some indication of job creation and sector-focus. The trend line for Ethiopia after 2011 and up to 2020 is very positive. Besides capital investment, there is also political investment from external actors who have been especially interested in the possibilities of the Abiy government. Winning the Nobel Prize in 2019 for formally ending the war with Eritrea earned Abiy a large amount of political goodwill, including from the US government (The Nobel Prize, 2019). But the promise of a second term as prime minister after his party won in June 2021 elections comes with new international and financial challenges. Inflation reached 34 percent in 2021 and liberalization efforts to privatize state firms have stalled. External public debt has soared and preferential trade agreements with the United States are threatened by the political violence unleashed by the prime minister's crackdown on rivals (Hudson, 2021). Clearly, access to lending and capital investment has not resolved some core political disagreements among Ethiopia's political factions; arguably it may have ignited more competition among rival political groups over access to resources and economic opportunity (or the old ways of consolidating political and economic advantage among groups).

When we compare across regions, among the major sources of investment and contracting, there has been a strong Chinese presence in Ethiopia,

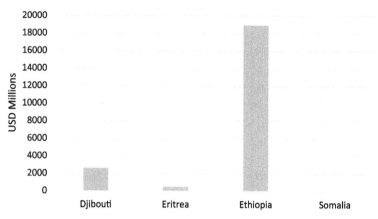

FIGURE 3.11 Chinese investment and contracting in Ethiopia, 2010–2019. *Source*: American Enterprise Institute Global China Investment Tracker.

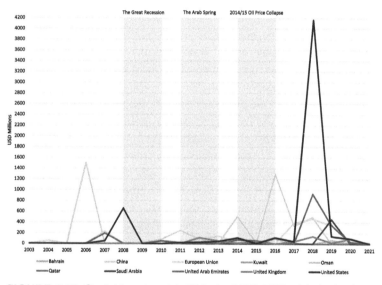

FIGURE 3.12 Capital investment in Ethiopia, 2003–2020, global selections. *Sources*: American Enterprise Institute, fDi Markets.

especially in contracting. But more interesting perhaps is the surge of American capital flows into Ethiopia in 2018, sending a strong signal of the country's liberalization outlook under the early Abiy administration.

The year 2018 becomes a high-water mark for Ethiopia's ability to attract foreign investment. But comparatively, again the combined weight of the GCC states as a source of investment in Ethiopia is strong and, in some ways, more consistent over time. Qatar emerges as a key investment origination point in 2008 and again a decade later. (Though Gulf interest also surges in the 2018 period.) When looking at total investment over the period 2014–2020 in Ethiopia from the GCC compared to China, the United States, or European Union as origination points, the GCC is only slightly behind China and surpasses the EU by more than $1 billion.

On job creation, a very different picture emerges in the capacity of Chinese investment in Ethiopia. China by far has created more jobs in Ethiopia than its US, European, or Gulf peer investors. Yet, there is also a sharp drop-off in the pivotal 2018–2019 period, as perhaps private capital begins to take on state capital as a source of investment, going from a high mark of 7,000 jobs in 2016 created by Chinese investment, to nearly 6,000 in 2018 to flatlining in 2019. The Covid-19 pandemic had a chilling effect on job creation from all investment sources in 2020.

When we examine the extent of UAE aid and investment in Ethiopia after 2018, there are several components. The government placed a $1 billion central bank deposit, which helped secure Ethiopia's balance of payments crisis and stabilize its currency. This worked in some ways in conjunction with support from international financial institutions,

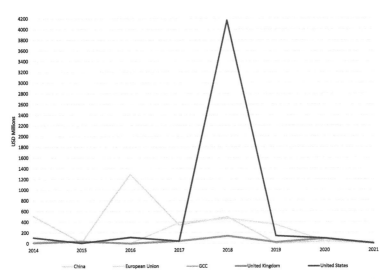

FIGURE 3.13 GCC compared to other key investment sources over time in Ethiopia, 2014–2020. *Sources*: American Enterprise Institute, fDi Markets.

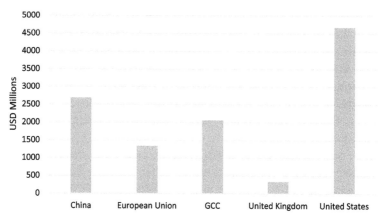

FIGURE 3.14 GCC compared to other key investment sources, totals, 2014–2020. *Sources*: American Enterprise Institute, fDi Markets.

somewhat similar to the 2016 package in Egypt that included Gulf support. In addition to the central bank deposit, the UAE committed to $2 billion in investments. Those investments are outlined below in what has actually materialized in the country and is reported by fDi Markets. (It is also possible some placements arrived but went unreported.) In institutional cooperation, the UAE signed a $100 million agreement to invest from its Khalifa Fund for Enterprise Development with the Ethiopian Ministry of Finance in 2018 (*The Economist*, 2019). While the sum of the fund is well below a $2 billion total investment ideal, it materializes and institutionalizes government economic development counterparts, with sectoral priorities and job creation goals.

One UAE investment in Ethiopia stands out in November 2018, on its timing, amount, and structure of ownership of the investor. Eagle Hills, a real estate developer based in Abu Dhabi, privately-held but understood to be under the leadership and personal ownership of members of the Abu Dhabi ruling family, invested $646.6 million in 2018 to build an apartment complex and retail space in central Addis Ababa. The firm is led by Mohamed Alabbar, also the chairman of Emaar Properties (which is a publicly listed firm) (Eagle Hills, n.d.). The real estate sector is frequently used as an investment vehicle of ruling family members, their investment holding companies, and state-owned entities that often overlaps with state foreign policy goals. Take, for example, the Emirati firm Aldar, which is owned in part by the sovereign wealth fund Mubadala (29 percent of shares in the publicly listed firm are owned by Mamoura

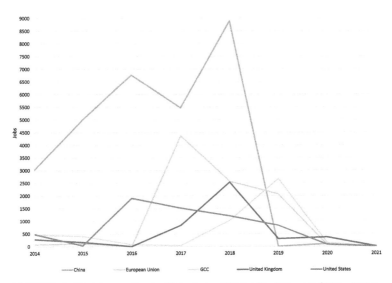

FIGURE 3.15 Job creation in Ethiopia by GCC, US, EU, and China, 2014–2020. *Sources*: American Enterprise Institute, fDi Markets.

Holding, which is now Mubadala Investment Company) as well as private local investors (Aldar, 2020; Sovereign Wealth Fund Institute, 2021). Aldar has been integral to the property development market in Egypt. In September 2021, Aldar partnered with ADQ to purchase in an all-cash offer, 90 percent of the share capital of Egypt's Sixth of October development company which has won government contracts to develop the new capital city, among other projects (Rahman, 2021). ADQ is an Abu Dhabi-based and government-owned holding company, whose chairman is Sheikh Tahnoon bin Zayed al Nahyan, also National Security Advisor and full brother to the Crown Prince, Mohamed bin Zayed.

In Ethiopia, the ability to deploy large amounts of capital toward real estate developments, partnered on both sides with government entities, displays a mechanism of development finance that has no equals among development finance institutions or multilateral banks. In the banking and finance sector in Ethiopia, there is poor access to capital through local bank lending and very little external experience among bankers with large project finance transactions. As the World Bank has argued:

Ethiopia's financial sector has, over the past decade, been operating under a financial repression framework used by the government for managing its monetary and foreign exchange policy, and financing of large infrastructure projects and state-owned enterprises (SOEs). Instruments used under this framework include the central bank financing of the government, a state-dominated banking sector, mandatory financing of priority projects and directed credit, administered interest rates, a captive domestic market for government debt, high liquidity and capital requirements, and strict foreign exchange controls. Over time, the framework has led to the build-up of large macro financial imbalances; these include a system of fiscal dominance, pressures on inflation, the overvaluation of the Birr, a chronic shortage of foreign exchange, the lack of development of the financial system, a credit allocation skewed toward the public sector, and an overall risk of malinvestment.

The World Bank, 2019

The World Bank's own assessment and effort at steering reforms in Ethiopia speak volumes to the challenge of a state-dominated economy. The central bank has tightly controlled foreign exchange accessibility, which in turn makes access to capital difficult. The structure of ownership within the bank sector is not completely state-owned, but because private banks are so captive to the government for access to foreign exchange, their flexibility in financing large projects is limited. And the process naturally leads to higher inflation.

However, the government of Ethiopia, and its Gulf supporters, might argue that this state-led investment strategy has seen some success. Despite the limits of capital movement, GDP growth averaged 10.4 percent in 2004–2018. Foreign direct investment increased from an average of $400 million between 2010 and 2012 to $3.7 billion in 2016 and 2018. Gross national income per capita increased from $140 in 2004 to $790 in 2018. A strong industrial policy that encouraged and solicited FDI into export sectors reaped some rewards in manufacturing, including in the auto sector. Forced investment into large government infrastructure created some results as well, with the share of the population with access to electricity tripling between 2004 and 2018, the share of the population with access to water doubled, and the availability of roads nearly quadrupled, all according to the World Bank's own assessment (The World Bank, 2019).

But the disadvantages are clear in limiting access to capital and how the state and its related firms crowd out opportunity for the private sector. The World Bank found that in Ethiopia the share of state-owned entity (SOE) credit increased from 14 percent of total outstanding bank loans in 2007 to 54 percent by 2018. And the World Bank found clear problems in businesses waiting for access to foreign exchange in order to close transactions, with reports of up to one year of a wait among many. This is very similar to bank sector allocations in the Gulf. Bank deposits and then also bank lending tends to be dominated by public sector or state-related entities. Looking across the GCC, public sector deposits are more than 20 percent of bank deposits in Saudi Arabia, and more than 30 percent of total deposits in Qatar (Young, 2020e). Because many banks are also partially owned by governments or members of ruling families, there is also a risk of moral hazard as competition for lending expands and governments may want to lean on local banks for support (*The Financial Times*, 2017). The risk to small and medium-sized enterprises (SME) becomes obvious, as prior to the Covid-19 crisis, lending to SMEs across the GCC was low. Between just 5 and 7 percent of bank loans went to such enterprises in Kuwait, Saudi Arabia, the UAE, and Oman, according to data from the IMF (2018). The implication is that in a financial crisis or an external shock, an economy without access to free capital movements and a healthy bank sector will be more vulnerable to a sharp recession, particularly if government spending and contracting freezes. Or more so in the case of Ethiopia, if external sources of support (especially central bank deposits in foreign currency) are extinguished.

Ethiopia's foreign ownership laws are also extreme, in that the laws discourage foreign direct investment in the bank sector. And despite some of the above-mentioned problems with the Gulf bank sector, it is a sector ready to expand and able to support foreign operations. Ethiopia's bank sector has been closed to foreign investors, but a 2019 law allows foreigners of "Ethiopian origin" the opportunity to invest, a policy geared toward the vibrant diaspora community in the United States and elsewhere.

To assess the role of the Gulf states, and in particular the role of the UAE in Ethiopia's efforts at liberalization and growth, especially in the period after 2018, we need some context. Ethiopia's regulatory environment for attracting investment was exceptionally poor. The fact that the UAE saw an opportunity to engage, both politically and economically, was more than many other states or private investors might have done. Though the presence of a spike in US investment in Ethiopia in 2018 speaks to that growth potential; but it was not repeated. So does the use of US trade incentives like the Africa Growth and Opportunity Act, which allowed a free trade agreement between Ethiopia and the

United States. The agreement facilitated $245 million in exports from Ethiopia to the US in 2020. But the US government suspended the trade agreement in November 2021 as a warning to the Ethiopian government over its use of violence and war against political and minority groups (Tadesse & Gebre, 2021).

Saudi Arabia has been more cautious in its investments in Ethiopia. There were just three prominent (over $100 million) investments in the period between 2009 and 2020, all made in 2019. These were two investments in renewable energy with ACWA Power and one in agribusiness/manufacturing from Midroc-Al Moudi, a Saudi-based firm with deep roots in Ethiopia from the Al Moudi family. Perhaps unrelatedly, Mohammed Hussein al-Amoudi was detained in the 2017 Ritz Carlton corruption purge and released in 2019 (Maasho & Kalin, 2019).

In 2019, ACWA Power, a Saudi-based water desalination and renewable energy developer, won contracts to build two solar power plants with a combined capacity to generate 250 megawatts of electricity. ACWA Power is partially owned by the Saudi Public Investment Fund; the sovereign wealth fund has gradually increased its stake to 50 percent in the power operator over several years and now uses the company as a somewhat exclusive provider of new solar projects through the kingdom (Nair & Martin, 2020). The agreement is one of the first under a public-private partnership law in that the state-owned utility Ethiopia Electric Power (EEP) would agree to a long-term power purchase agreement at a set price of 2.25 cents per kilowatt hour for twenty years (Clarion Energy, 2019). The new power plants are based in the Dicheto, Afar region and in Gad, Somali region. The deal is worth about $330 million according to fDi Markets, but the structure is the most important aspect of this agreement. Two state-owned or state-related entities align interests to regenerate revenue in a long-term, relatively low-risk agreement. The power developer gets a foothold in renewable production in a highly populated growing economy, whose electricity needs will only grow. Saudi Arabia increases its ability to provide development finance opportunities through a profit-driven company with lots of runway for the kingdom's aspirations in the renewable energy business.

Qatar has been largely absent as an investor or source of aid in Ethiopia in the period between 2015 and 2020. Its interests have been focused elsewhere among the cases in this study. Oman and Pakistan figure prominently, compared to Qatar's near exit from Egypt, and small engagements in Sudan, Jordan, and Lebanon, comparatively.

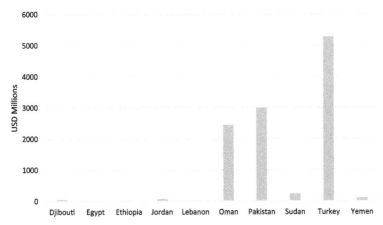

FIGURE 3.16 Qatar financial investment and support into case countries, 2015–2020. *Sources*: American Enterprise Institute, fDi markets.

Where the Saudi and Emirati positions in support of the Abiy government in Ethiopia have differed is in the level (by quantity of projects and amount of projects) of foreign direct investment, and direct central bank support (by UAE and not Saudi Arabia). Both have relied upon by state-related or linked entities in investment commitments. Where they also converged is in diplomatic efforts to broker a peace agreement between Ethiopia and Eritrea in 2018, which were successful (Ministry of Information Eritrea, 2018). The degree to which either external actor tipped the balance is unclear. And this type of intervention at the diplomatic level, reinforced with aid and investment commitments may not occur again, given Ethiopia's slide into political violence in 2020–2021. In an affirmation of the learning that has occurred since 2018, a senior Emirati official overseeing a state investment vehicle described the UAE has "trying to play a quiet and constructive role" in 2021, in a much lower profile effort (Anon., 2021).

Conclusion

In the cases of Egypt and Ethiopia, these are best case scenarios for intervention, in that these are economies with strong growth trajectories, demographic dividends (in that their youthful populations are poised to continue consumer growth and workforce development increases in skills), and their governments have been open to foreign assistance. In the case of Egypt, the revolution in 2011 and the counter-revolution in 2013 generated space for a number of external actors to enter Egyptian political and economic decision-making. This period will probably be known as the beginning of a post-American era in the Middle East, as the democracy promotion of Western liberal states and their accompanying financial institutions ended with less influence in the outcome of the Egyptian political economy than the actions of regional states, most importantly Qatar, the UAE, and Saudi Arabia. As for institutional outcomes, the most prominent example is a reinforcement of state-owned real estate development and urban planning that imagines more for the role of government ministries and bureaucracy than for centers for new business or innovation. But despite this well-known understanding of the role of the Egyptian military and state-connected firms in many new projects, including the new capital city, the Egyptian economy has seen significant growth, especially in its equity markets. The dual track of reforms and exemptions pursued in Egypt under Sisi exemplify this contradiction. While Gulf support for an IMF package helped push through a number of structural necessary reforms, including a value-added tax (VAT) implementation, there were large carve-outs for state-linked firms. For example, the military and security institutions were exempt from the VAT. The military does not pay VAT on goods, equipment, machinery, services, and raw materials used for defense and national security—and arguably for contracts awarded domestically (Reuters, 2018).

In Ethiopia, one could argue progress has been made, and even encouraged by the opportunity of Gulf-backed investment, especially in the case of private-public partnerships in electricity and utility awards. But clearly there has been little push for expansion of the rights of smaller firms for access to capital and competition, in spite of the US effort to secure a free trade avenue for Ethiopian exports. The Abiy government proved the economic incentives of FDI inflows, preferential trade policy, and direct support to its monetary policy were not enough to change the government's course in limiting participation and rights of political rivals.

These two cases are not exactly examples of state capitalism, but rather of a capitalism restrained, with some reforms in subsidy reduction, tax implementation, and opening to foreign ownership, but also some major advantages for the duration to accommodate and maintain central political authority. These cases may be more of an indication of where the future of South-South development institutional ties are headed. Infrastructure investment is a priority, and it does do substantial good in delivering services to citizens and opening opportunity—to a point. Job creation in both cases has been very volatile and often tied to the large projects of the state. Egypt is a case of very good access to external funding, including debt capital markets externally and in its domestic bank system. Ethiopia has been less advantaged.

The next chapter examines similar difficulties in access to credit where China has played an important role. In this chapter and the next, what emerges is a story of increasing options for developing economies in the path to growth, and the paradox of how more points of access to infrastructure lending and contracting has led to fewer pathways to broader structural reform and room for economic competition.

4 CAUGHT BETWEEN THE GULF AND CHINA: CASE STUDIES OF FINANCIAL INTERVENTION IN OMAN AND PAKISTAN

Oman and Pakistan have experienced a different kind of Gulf financial intervention. These are states where we see a strong domestic political and security rationale for engagement from the Gulf. There is certainly also a link to energy markets and Gulf domestic economic interests, especially in the case of Pakistan, but the political and security relationship has probably weighed more heavily. For Oman, the politics within the Gulf Cooperation Council (GCC) have added to stresses on the availability of committed fiscal support since 2011. The Qatar crisis from June 2017 to January 2021 also affected Oman, as has the civil war and Saudi-led intervention in Yemen. For Pakistan, the security relationship and military ties with Saudi Arabia have been both a source of tension and also a reason for financial support and investment. As with Oman, the Saudi military intervention in Yemen has been a source of strain in the Saudi-Pakistani relationship. These are also two states that sit geographically at an eastern port and outpost, so to speak, of Gulf interests and in the growing importance of eastward ties to Asia. In terms of access to finance and the growing leverage of China as a key consumer in energy markets, Oman and Pakistan have found themselves caught between the development ambitions of the Gulf and China.

This chapter examines how Gulf and Chinese financial intervention works sometimes in synergy and sometimes in competition in recipient states. The co-investments in the energy sector by both Gulf and Chinese state oil companies are one example. In Oman and Pakistan, we see the Chinese Belt and Road Initiative in its full ambitions, but also the overlap of Gulf energy transition goals and some inter-Gulf rivalry, a part of the sub-regional dimension of Gulf foreign policy. Both cases also illustrate the difficulty developing countries find when they are in need of external finance, and how traditional sources of loans and debt issuance in private markets are often not available or insufficient, making state-led development finance solutions more attractive. In Pakistan, we see the corporatization of Gulf financial intervention, using Gulf state-owned oil companies as sources of investment, but also strategic positioning of assets within an energy value chain, from refineries to petrochemical facilities. Likewise, the ability to reward and award states with access to their own mechanisms of revenue generation is indeed a tool of economic statecraft. The Abu Dhabi National Oil Company awarded the Pakistani government oil company a concession to drill for oil in the UAE in the summer of 2021, in a tender that saw many international oil companies surprised to see competition from a much smaller state-owned firm (Saadi, 2021).

Aid and Investment Flows from the GCC to Pakistan

First, let the data speak. Looking first at foreign direct investment flows, there is clearly a strong preference for Pakistan over other destinations included in this study, and not just a preference from the Gulf states, but from other sources as well. Pakistan is an important emerging market and destination for investment flows for its population size and its geography. Its outsize military spending and capacity is also a draw. China has been a consistent source of investment and economic activity in Pakistan over the last fifteen years, but spikes in investment from China are visible from 2014 onward and represent a heightened interest from China in its Belt and Road Initiative. China has been an active investor and contractor in Pakistan for over a decade. But the position of the Pakistani economy *vis-à-vis* other emerging market opportunities is worth some contextualization.

Pakistan has had good access to development finance and aid and is the beneficiary of large flows of remittances from its citizens working in

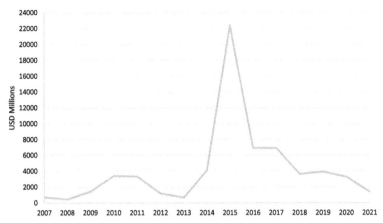

FIGURE 4.1 Chinese investment and contracting in Pakistan, 2007–2021. *Source*: American Enterprise Institute Global China Investment Tracker.

the Gulf and further abroad. Greenfield investment flows and new foreign direct investment are not necessarily a primary source of capital flows in Pakistan, but those sources of FDI are predominantly from China and the Gulf states. From international financial institutions, Pakistan has relied on support packages from the International Monetary Fund and for large project finance from the World Bank, especially concessional financing through the Bank's Multilateral Investment Guarantee Agency (MIGA). MIGA provides a means of obtaining insurance cover against non-commercial risks. Pakistan is a top beneficiary of the MIGA investment cover. Historically, and particularly through the 1990s, MIGA provided Pakistan with 9.4 percent of its investment insurance facilities, the highest among developing countries (Khan & Kim, 1999).

Two key differences in the political economy of Pakistan versus Oman, for example, are in its flexible exchange rate and in its use of external financial support through the IMF and World Bank. Oman has been classified more as a middle-income country, without the same access to concessionary finance. Yet, as Oman's exposure to a higher external public debt to GDP ratio increases, it begins to look more like an economy like Pakistan's with a higher dependence on external sources of financial support to continue government expected outlays. Oman's credit rating has also been downgraded so that it approaches more of Pakistan's debt profile globally in the last five years. Even as government economic reform efforts have steamed ahead in Oman under Sultan Haitham, the outlook for Oman looks more like that of a lower-middle income economy than a wealthy petrostate.

Continuing on Pakistan's economic outlook, the country has benefitted from access to international financial institutions along with significant inflows from both China and the Gulf states. But the intersection of trade flows from China and the health of the Chinese economy, along with the fluctuations in oil prices make Pakistan vulnerable to the global economy in more direct ways from its two key sources of investment. When we track capital investment into Pakistan from the GCC states, China, member states of the European Union, the United Kingdom, and the United States from 2003–2021, a very clear picture emerges in the dominance of the GCC and China as sources of investment. Job creation follows the same pattern.

Foreign aid is as important, if not more important, as a source of inflows in Pakistan historically. And the effectiveness of aid in Pakistan is intriguing, as Pakistan has reduced its poverty headcount by nearly 66 percent between 2002 and 2016, despite poor governance, weak institutions, mediocre economic growth, and poor social indicators, as some scholars argue (Afzal et al., 2021).

The United States has been a strong source of foreign and often military aid to Pakistan, especially since 2001. Data from the US government source, www.foreignassistance.gov, finds that of US aid to Pakistan since 2001, 54 percent has been allocated to military assistance and 46 percent to economic assistance. In the period between 2001 and 2021, there is a high point of assistance in 2010, with $2.61 billion

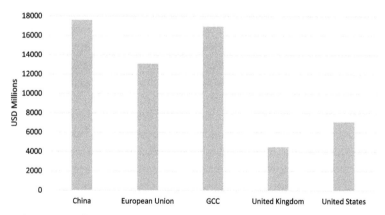

FIGURE 4.2 Capital investment in Pakistan, 2003–2021. *Sources*: American Enterprise Institute, fDi Markets.

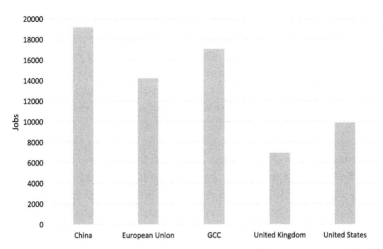

FIGURE 4.3 Jobs created in Pakistan, 2003–2021. *Sources*: American Enterprise Institute, fDi Markets.

$684,764,240

ALL AGENCIES: $685M

2001

2022

Partially reported year(s): 2021, 2022

FIGURE 4.4 US foreign assistance to Pakistan, 2001–2021. *Source*: https://www.foreignassistance.gov/cd/pakistan/

allocated. For comparison, in 2019, US aid to Pakistan totaled just over $684 million. The aftermath of the 9/11 attacks and the US war on terror justified the aid expenditure from the US government perspective, and it also probably delayed consideration of aid tied more closely to governance reforms.

By the same token, one might argue that external support, through remittances and targeted state investments have made dents in poverty reduction at the community level without interfering or disrupting governance practices, for better or worse. This could be one indication of the influence of state capitalism at work; but disaggregating aid from liberal democracies would prove difficult and seems to have had the same effects. In the World Bank's 2021 economic assessment of Pakistan, the bank finds that during the first half of fiscal year 2021, the current account recorded a surplus of $1.1 billion (compared to a $2 billion deficit in the first half of 2020), which was the first surplus in a decade (The World Bank, 2021a, p. 17). The bank's assessment is that despite a wider trade deficit, record remittance inflows pushed the current account balance to the black in this difficult period. The resilience of remittance flows in the crisis of the pandemic, speaks to the country's vulnerability to regional downturns in the Gulf, and the willingness of expatriate citizens to increase transfers at moments of crisis. Remittances grew by about 25 percent to reach a record US$14.2 billion between 2020 and the first half of 2021 (The World Bank, 2021a, p. 10). Despite lower direct investment and portfolio flows, debt financing from bilateral, multilateral (namely, an IMF support package), and commercial banks supported the financial account, which recorded an overall net inflow during this period.

Taking a closer look at the kinds of capital investment and direct bilateral support committed from the Gulf states to Pakistan, another trend line emerges. Bilateral support from the Gulf states ties in very closely to political and security demands, ramping up after 2015. From China, investments move into new sectors like renewable power and communications from more traditional sectors like construction, manufacturing (rubber), and oil and gas after 2015. These movements are aligned, but originate from very different sets of strategic interests.

A timeline of key events in Gulf-Pakistan relations of the last twenty years provides some indication of this progression of interest and priorities. Saudi-Pakistani economic and security ties predate this recent period; some scholars point to the period after the 1973 oil embargo and 1979 Iranian revolution and siege in Mecca as milestones for the initial cementing of ties. Continually, Pakistan has balanced between its relationship with Iran and the Gulf Arab states (Siddiqi, 2019).

2001: Post 9/11: Pakistan had supported the Taliban in Afghanistan up until 2001 with goals of increasing stable trade opportunities in the region and having a pro-Pakistan government as a neighbor; this position had backfired on Pakistan throughout the 1990s, and they reversed the policy on September 12. Pakistan almost immediately became the hub for international aid and rebuilding efforts in the region and secured $1.5 billion in US direct assistance or grants within four months.

2001: The Kingdom of Saudi Arabia (KSA) and Pakistan announce joint project to manufacture light arms and ammunition.

2004: Pakistan and GCC sign Framework Agreement on Economic Cooperation, as first step toward liberalization and potential free trade agreement.

2005: Earthquakes in Pakistan; KSA and UAE respond with reconstruction aid, as well as medical supplies; Saudis pledged $133 million direct aid grant, $187 million concessional loans, and $153 million export credits.

2006: Oman and Pakistan put on elaborate naval exercises and establish the Pakistan-Oman Joint Program Review Group to plan defensive cooperation.

2006: Pakistan-UAE Defense Cooperation Agreement signed.

2006: Kashmir conflict, GCC states aim to remain neutral.

2007: Pakistani President Musharraf attended Arab League summit in Riyadh even though Pakistan did not yet have "observer member" status.

2008: Bahrain and Pakistan commit to increasing defense cooperation.

2008: IMF grants $7.6 billion loan to Pakistan with 23-month term, with conditions of reducing the deficit and inflation, and increasing the social safety net for the poor through cash transfers. $3.1 billion of the loan was made available immediately.

2010: Worst floods in eighty years kill 1600; government response widely criticized. Financial aid in response is significantly lower than previous crises; of GCC states, only Kuwait and KSA pledged more than $5 million in aid (as did Britain, US, Australia, and Italy).

2011: IMF loan of $11.3 billion expires when Pakistan fails to implement conditions attached to it, including broadening the country's tax base and privatizing state-owned companies (Anwar, 2011).

2012: Iran-Pakistan pipeline project is announced to start, slated to be finished in 2014. (The pipeline was not completed by 2021.)

2013: IMF approves $6.7 billion loan package for Pakistan with a 36-month term.

2015: Prime Minister Nawaz Sharif declares neutrality in the Yemen crisis, codified in a resolution passed by Pakistan's parliament. The resolution notably called for neutrality "so as to be able to play a proactive diplomatic role to end the crisis."

2015: China and Pakistan sign agreements worth billions of dollars to boost infrastructure, designed to end Pakistan's energy crises and turn the country into regional economic hub, termed "China Pakistan Economic Corridor"; China pledged roughly $60 billion in investment in Pakistan as part of the Belt and Road Initiative

2018: KSA announces $6.2 billion package to Pakistan, including $3 billion in loans and $3.2 billion oil credit facility.

2019: IMF support package to Pakistan of $6 billion.

2019: Qatar announces $3 billion in support to Pakistan, combined central bank deposit and FDI commitment.

2019: Mohammed bin Salman visit to Pakistan, commitment of $20 billion in investments

This list of aid commitments and strategic engagement between Pakistan and the Gulf Arab states (and Iran) is interspersed with the receipt of significant external finance from the IMF. And toward the late 2010s, Pakistan begins more direct financial integration with China. Pakistan is clearly pulled in different directions and increasingly reliant on multiple sources for its development and growth agenda. In his book, *The Dragon from the Mountains* (2021), McCartney situates Pakistan and China's economic corridor into a global perspective of major infrastructure investments and partnerships, and it is certainly an historic one. As McCartney writes, "the promised long-term commitment from China to Pakistan dwarfes any other foreign relationship for Pakistan since independence" (2021, p. 5). But, the Chinese interest in Pakistan is certainly predated and rests alongside a more dynamic set of linkages, both security and ideological, with Saudi Arabia.

Saudi-Pakistani ties align more with both states' identity and legitimacy formations. Both countries work together at the international level, including within the Organization of Islamic Cooperation. Saudi Arabia is a key labor market partner for Pakistan, hosting nearly 2 million Pakistani guest workers. Since 2016, many of those guest workers in construction have been leaving the kingdom, forced out by redundancies and a major restructuring of the two largest Saudi contracting firms, Saudi Oger and Bin Laden Group (Young, 2016a).

But it is the security relationship and close ties with Pakistan's military that make it so important to Saudi Arabia. Saudi Arabia has made it clear that it has civilian nuclear power ambitions and would want nuclear weapons on parity with its regional rival Iran, should Iran produce them (MEED, 2021; Shalev, 2012). Saudi Arabia is actively moving toward nuclear power generation and has continued to move toward that capacity without agreeing to the same terms for nuclear material storage and disposal that define the UAE's "gold standard" pact with the United States (US Government Accoutability Office, 2020). Pakistan's nuclear program for military use is a core attraction, but its large military and advisory capacity has been useful to Saudi Arabia, though not necessarily as reliable as it may have hoped. Pakistani military personnel often serve in Saudi Arabia, including as part of the Islamic Military Counter Terrorism Coalition, formed in 2017 with a former Pakistani commander, Raheel Sharif as its head (Gul, 2017). Saudi Arabia hosts other militaries in advisory capacity, notably from the United States, but the Pakistani cooperation has extended to troops stationed in the kingdom. This presence is related or even concessionary, given Pakistan's positioning between Iran and Saudi Arabia in the Yemen conflict. The sticking point came with the invitation for Pakistan to contribute to the Saudi-led war effort in Yemen. Pakistan baulked, which elicited one of the strongest push-backs from the Gulf Arab states, including a condemnation from the UAE for Pakistan's reluctance in April 2015 (Al Arabiya News, 2015b).

Among the Gulf states, Pakistan presents different opportunities and potential for collaboration. For Saudi Arabia, this has traditionally been a security and military linkage, but that is also joined most recently in energy cooperation and new investments into petrochemical and refinery capacity in Pakistan. For the UAE, there has been a security relationship and long-standing cultural ties in Pakistan (e.g., royal hunting trips) (Baloch, 2021). But the UAE has been a more important source of incoming investment to Pakistan than other Gulf states. The UAE is generally a larger source of outflows throughout the MENA and Horn regions than its GCC co-members. In Table 4.1, we see exactly how the UAE is a force more in line with China and the European Union as an active source of investment in Pakistan, and competitively since the early 2000s.

TABLE 4.1 Capital investment in Pakistan, 2003–2021 (in US$ millions)

												Capital Investment
Year	Bahrain	China	European Union	Kuwait	Oman	Qatar	Saudi Arabia	United Arab Emirates	United Kingdom	United States
2003	0	466	660	0	0	0	0	35	0	309
2004	0	32	1	61	0	70	150	6	172	743
2005	0	358	385	0	0	0	200	577	495	121
2006	0	268	555	0	0	0	0	1366	1069	90
2007	0	400	86	0	0	0	0	1390	0	402
2008	35	131	323	0	0	0	265	1076	139	3191
2009	0	0	2076	0	0	0	1839	493	10	16
2010	0	535	93	0	0	0	35	70	64	310
2011	174	75	63	0	0	3	0	897	46	147
2012	0	0	1951	0	0	0	0	55	35	16
2013	0	170	259	0	0	19	56	37	56	166
2014	0	4729	1825	0	0	3	31	122	8	9

Year										
2015	258	7194	927	0	0	0	0	5594	1840	46
2016	0	310	1031	971	0	0	0	17	192	212
2017	0	1889	132	0	0	0	0	58	149	238
2018	31	288	255	0	0	0	0	929	177	939
2019	0	617	2303	0	0	0	6	0	14	102
2020	0	0	147	0	0	0	6	0	21	17
2021	0	120	4	0	0	0	0	0	0	8
Total	497.40	17582.80	13075.81	1032.70	0.00	95.10	2586.70	12723.30	4487.35	7083.00

Sources: American Enterprise Institute, fDi Markets.

Looking at the last six years, from 2014–2020, there is another pattern that emerges. The GCC states and China look more aligned in their investment trends toward Pakistan. Figure 4.5 represents these flows.

China's economic interests in Pakistan accelerate in this period in the 2010s as well, as a direct feature of the New Silk Road or Belt and Road Initiative. The China-Pakistan economic corridor is a key conduit of China's outward trade and investment strategy. Chinese lending to Pakistan in this period is probably more important than its investment. The use of state-owned banks as a lever of influence is quite different from concessional finance from international development banks or institutions. China's use of this kind of tool accelerated in the 2010s, in some ways for its own domestic interests to build the balance sheets of its own banks, but in political ways to build influence in its expansionary plans for regional economic integration.

Chinese lending to Pakistan increased with the announcement of the joint economic corridor, but immediately led to an opportunity for Chinese banks to provide capital. In 2017, Chinese financial institutions lent $1.2 billion, half from the government run China Development Bank and half from the state-owned Industrial Commercial Bank of China

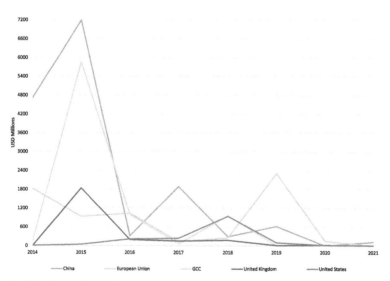

FIGURE 4.5 Capital investment in Pakistan from the EU, US, UK, China, and GCC, 2014–2020 (in US$ millions). *Sources*: American Enterprise Institute, fDi Markets.

(Stacey et al., 2017). Another $2 billion in loans followed in 2018 (Marlow et al., 2018). Then $3.5 billion in a loan in 2019 (Gul, 2019). The pattern has continued. The total expected lending from China to Pakistan for the economic corridor amounts to $60 billion. There is no other line of credit for emerging market sovereigns that, at the outset, commits to such a trajectory.

For China, Pakistan becomes an important economic client, and not just for Chinese banks. Following research from the Stockholm International Peace Research Institute reported by Bloomberg, arms sales from China to Pakistan have displaced the US in value since 2010 (Marlow et al., 2018). China's military sales are an important source of revenue and political influence. Sales to Pakistan have been consistent for over a decade, while the US has diminished its arms exports to Pakistan. In this sense, the linkage of financial leverage with growing security ties and strategic interests for China's own expansionist goals is very similar to how Saudi Arabia has seen its bilateral relationship with Pakistan. China has more capacity for lending. But Saudi Arabia has used the same tool with arguably less commercial and more conciliatory terms over a longer period. Saudi loans to Pakistan have often been forgiven. One difference is that Saudi Arabia does not use state-owned banks for bilateral loans of this kind. The loan is directly from the government or ministry of finance. One question will be if Gulf economic statecraft begins to lever its bank sector in the way China has done. For now, that is not the case, although it is not unusual for governments in the Gulf through their various state-owned investment vehicles to be part owners of local banks. But Gulf financial intervention strategies and Chinese interventions are on converging trajectories.

These trajectories meet in the energy sector in Pakistan. The shared interest of Gulf hydrocarbon exporters and China's demand for energy and control over major logistical intersections or hubs along its Belt and Road Initiative mean that Pakistan is an essential entrepot (Rakhmat, 2019). There are some shared projects that mark this convergence. Examples are investment in pipelines, refinery and petrochemical facilities in Pakistan. China Petroleum Engineering and Construction (CPECC) signed a $317 million contract with Pakistan's Pak-Arab Refinery to build an oil product pipeline in December 2021. A subsidiary of the China National Petroleum Corp (CNPC) will manage engineering and construction of the project and the Import and Export Bank of China provided credit to the CPECC for the project (Reuters, 2002). The

Pak-Arab Refinery (PARCO) is jointly owned by the Government of Pakistan (with 60 percent of shares) and the Emirate of Abu Dhabi, through its sovereign wealth fund Mubadala (with 40 percent of shares) (Mubadala Investment Company, n.d.). Abu Dhabi has further strengthened ties to Pakistan via energy with a concession to a consortium of Pakistani oil firms for exploration and production in an offshore site, the first of its kind in 2021. That concession included fully government-owned entities in Pakistan, companies which have not won awards of this type in the UAE or the Gulf in the past (Kulovic, 2021).

But when governments manage market decisions, there are sometimes snags. For example, the Saudi $20 billion investment commitment in Pakistan included the construction of a $10 billion refinery and petrochemical facility to be built in Gwadar, the center of the China-Pakistan economic corridor. In 2021, the plan shifted to move the project closer to Karachi, as feasibility studies by Aramco did not find the port facility a good match for the proposed investment (Asian News International, 2021). These projects directly test the model of state-led growth in energy and infrastructure, not just for domestic development but in transferable models by design. There are clearly political goals in the awards, and sometimes the political goals override the economic incentives. And, like the global art market, sometimes there are project awards and transactions that reflect payment in-kind for a different service rendered or simply to build leverage for the future.

Gulf Financial Intervention in Oman

Oman's economic development has been jumpstarted under its new leadership of Sultan Haitham since 2020. But the underlying challenges of creating employment, attracting investment, finding new industries to replace or complement diminishing oil revenue, and the ability to service substantial sovereign debt are not new. Oman has relied on its GCC neighbors for financial support for decades, but the 2011 Arab uprisings created a mutual interest in quelling possible civil unrest and demands for economic and political reform in the council of monarchies. A threat in Oman was interpreted as a threat to all, as the same scenario played out violently in Bahrain.

While Saudi Arabia and the UAE sent troops and military support to Bahrain in 2011, Oman was the recipient of more economic modes of intervention. Omani domestic politics have seen occasional protests on economic issues, but the notion of external military support for domestic repression or stabilization is not welcome. Oman keeps a certain distance from its GCC neighbors, in its more neutral foreign policy which has been distinct historically in its relations with Iran and also with Israel. Oman and the UAE have at times been suspicious of each other, with tensions over surveillance and espionage surfacing occasionally in both 2011 and 2019 (BBC, 2011; Sheline, 2020). So while Oman has been the recipient of large amounts of GCC support, there is also a degree of hesitancy.

The timing of the Gulf support package of 2011 then led into a period of reconfiguration in GCC political economies. The oil price collapse in late 2014 created momentum to economic diversification plans the six Gulf Arab states had given lip-service to for years. This economic pressure, amid a very real challenge to governance across the Middle East, changed how Gulf states behaved on fiscal policy and especially on their willingness to borrow to finance ever larger deficits. It was a difficult time in the Gulf to leverage public resources to meet growing demand for jobs, for infrastructure development, and efforts to build economies less reliant on oil revenues (Young, 2018c). For those officials engaged in seeking external finance, either through debt or in foreign direct investment, finding the right partners becomes more difficult given regional political tensions and the urgency to bridge fiscal deficits and continue project pipelines. Oman exemplifies the challenges of generating investment and infrastructure growth with diminishing fiscal resources (Young, 2017b).

The Omani strategy has been two-fold: (1) to borrow out of a fiscal deficit, and (2) to approach structural reforms with caution, especially given the impact on cost of living and job growth. There is a palpable anxiety among policy advisors about the impact of austerity, and rather than reversing austerity measures (as Saudi Arabia did twice in the course of 2017), Oman has tried to concentrate on strategic communications with citizens about the nature of reforms and their immediate impact (Paul, 2017). In the case of reductions in fuel subsidies, the government created a direct transfer scheme to help low-income citizens pay for rising fuel costs (Mukrashi, 2017). And with mounting pressure to create more public sector employment for nationals, one can appreciate the prioritization of stability (Shaibany, 2018).

Ministers and economic advisors in Oman emphasized the need to generate growth and further long-term investment initiatives, even at the expense of a ballooning deficit and forgoing regional trends of tax implementation and subsidy reform. Oman did move toward budget tightening and tax implementation, but well after stability under Sultan Haitham was secured in 2020 (PwC, 2020). Oman was slower than its GCC peers in embracing fiscal reforms and relied heavily on debt after 2014 to maintain social spending.

Since early 2017, Oman has issued large amounts of debt and borrowed heavily in international bank loans. In March 2017, Oman issued $5 billion in international bonds, followed by a $2 billion sukuk in June (The Middle East North Africa Financial Network, 2017). In August 2017, the country borrowed $3.55 billion from Chinese banks (Reuters, 2017c). In January 2018, Oman went to bond markets again to issue $6.5 billion in dollar-denominated debt. The government announced plans to finance a new infrastructure fund through bank loans of as much as $1 billion (Carvalho, 2018). The appetite in 2018 seemed insatiable, as Oman announced plans to issue more international bonds for as much as $2 billion (Martin & Narayanan, 2018). The repayment of these loans and bonds, however, has already begun to limit fiscal flexibility.

Oman's budget deficit reached $2.9 billion in the first half of 2021, the equivalent of 8.5 percent of GDP on an annual basis. To finance that deficit, Oman borrowed 3.4 billion Omani riyals (or 12 percent of 2021 GDP) through loans and a drawdown on its sovereign wealth fund, the Oman Investment Authority (HSBC, 2021). The government has increasingly relied on the Omani private bank sector for credit. Under Sultan Haitham, the Omani government also began some long-overdue privatization sales of state assets and consolidated its oil and gas business into a new business unit, Energy Development Oman (EDO). And like Saudi Arabia, the ability to garner state revenue from tax has drastically shifted its non-oil revenue capacity.

The borrowing spree after 2015 was precipitated by the oil price collapse, but it established a pattern of fiscal governance that has been hard to break in the transition under new leadership. Moreover, the events of the six years following 2015 have not made access to external finance easier for Oman. The GCC dispute put Oman between Qatar on one side and Saudi Arabia and the UAE on the other. Tensions escalating with Iran under the Trump Administration made Omani foreign policy and potential trade with Iran off limits. And then the Covid-19 pandemic limited access to foreign currency revenues through tourism and severely limited domestic mobility. The government's efforts to create private sector jobs for nationals and to limit its exposure to the public sector wage bill came just before the pandemic, making new job creation all the more difficult. According to a 2021 government bond prospectus, census data from December 2019 showed Omanis constituted 21.3 percent of the labor force while foreigners, who make up 42.5 percent of the total population, made up 78.7 percent of the labor force. Omanis were 85.2 percent of government employees and only 16.1 percent of the private sector workforce, despite a hiring freeze on new public sector positions. The hiring freeze shifted the public sector wage bill from 12.4 percent of GDP in 2017 to approximately 11.4 percent of GDP in 2019 (Oman Sovereign Sukuk S.A.O.C., 2021).

Debt allowed the government to move forward with development plans that pre-date the decline in oil revenues, as well as regional tensions among GCC neighbors (Young, 2017c). While Oman saw an increase in port traffic and trade flows since June 2017, its airport expansion and strategic port projects like Duqm were well underway before the severing of trade ties with Qatar by the UAE, Saudi Arabia, and Bahrain. The airport project was funded by the $10 billion GCC support fund, a direct result of the 2011 uprisings (Laessing & Johnston, 2011). These investments will take years to generate the wealth the country hopes to find in new logistics, manufacturing and energy projects; a short-term proof of concept in the uptick Omani ports volume (due to the restrictions against Qatar) has served to justify some of the on-going expense of capital raising in a time of shortfall. The port of Sohar is an important case in point, as it has been designed as a free-zone to attract foreign direct investment as well as a logistics hub (SOHAR, n.d.). It serves long-term development needs for Oman, including job creation via automobile assembly plants, smelters and oil refineries, and agricultural depots for food security (for Oman, but potentially for regional neighbors like India as well) (*Muscat Daily*, 2018). And Sohar is a small project compared with the ambitious new industrial city underway at Duqm.

In Duqm, financing has been heavily reliant on China, with smaller investments from GCC neighbors (Jabarkhyl, 2017). The China-Oman Industrial Park in Duqm is a custom-made city within a special economic zone, expected to cost $10.7 billion, and to be financed through Chinese companies and bank loans (Business Gateways, 2017). The park plans to produce cars (a "high-mobility SUV"), solar panels, petrochemicals, oil field supplies, and have its own electricity and desalination plants. Saudi Arabia has made an effort to support the project, with a small $200 million part-grant/part-loan financing to fund road construction and a fishing harbor (Offshore Energy, 2018). A 30:70 joint investment between the Oman Investment fund (a sovereign wealth fund of Oman) and the Qatar Transport fund (signed in 2016) will establish a bus assembly plant at Duqm, worth 160 million Omani riyal ($416 million) (Sundar, 2019). Masdar, the UAE government-owned entity, invested in a major wind power farm in Oman, bridging its expertise in regional renewable projects; the farm began generating electricity in 2019 (Masdar, 2019). Its state-owned entity OQ, partnered with a consortium of investors, including Kuwait's Enertech, to create a green hydrogen facility (Ratcliffe, 2018).

While the ports and industrial zone projects are heavily reliant on foreign bonds and bank loans, there is also an effort to streamline the government's investment portfolio. Oman is a country in which the government plays the most significant role in capital expenditure and investment in the domestic economy. The government, through its various investment funds, like Tanmia, and individually through ministries, mandates most of the development opportunities in the country. A prime example is its ministry of defense and pension fund, which are major property-owners and developers, with assets like high-end hotels in the sultanate (*Times of Oman*, 2021).

The government follows a five-year development strategy (and has used five-year plans for decades) and has been engaged in its own "national transformation" for economic diversification, with changes to managerial practice within ministries, including meeting key performance indicator targets within the Tanfeedh program (Omanuna, n.d.). Combining government investments funds and streamlining the multiple ministerial stakeholders in local development projects has meant disrupting practices of rent-seeking, and inefficient management. There are new efforts to streamline these various funds, particularly in tourism investments so that outside partners might help shoulder some of the cost (and reap the benefit) of domestic economic development plans, as in the Omran fund (Nair & Narayanan, 2017). In the summer of 2020, a royal decree by Sultan Haitham created a new sovereign wealth fund, the Oman Investment Authority (OIA), the newly-formed sovereign wealth fund that is made from the Oman State General Reserve Fund, Oman Investment Fund, and other entities. The estimated $17 billion sovereign wealth fund merged some state-owned enterprises and created new government businesses (Sovereign Wealth Fund Institute, 2021). This fund is modeled on Abu Dhabi, and perhaps even a Malaysian approach to state-led investment vehicles (Bank Nizwa, 2021).

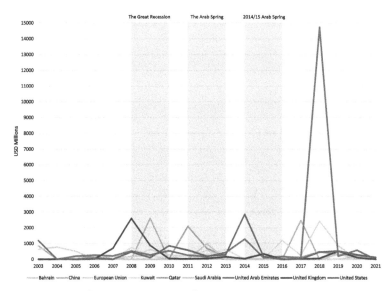

FIGURE 4.6 Capital investment in Oman, various sources, 2003–2021 (in US$ millions). *Sources*: American Enterprise Institute, fDi Markets.

Policy choices have lasting consequences, and it will probably be a decade or more before we can look back on this period of relative austerity in the GCC, when public finance finally gave way to impose taxes, reduce the bloated public wage bill, and seek external funding to bridge deficits and support new growth. The new owners of infrastructure, including new power plants, ports and manufacturing zones, are determined now. Who the bondholders and lenders will be, those who can influence future policy choices, is also important, particularly as we can expect some refinancing in the near-term. Refinancing the terms of a multi-billion dollar loan with a state-linked Chinese bank could be a bit more complex. Time has been the most pressing determinant of Oman's financing requirements, and those lenders and partners who have been willing to step in quickly have been rewarded with favorable terms and access. China and Gulf neighbors the United Arab Emirates and Qatar have all been active in Oman.

In Figures 4.7–4.9, we see how select cases are dominant in Gulf financial aid and intervention, and for the UAE and Qatar, how Pakistan and Oman have both received significant resources. But it is the UAE that accelerated its intervention in Oman between 2017 and 2019. Figure 4.10

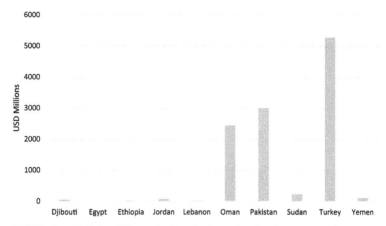

FIGURE 4.7 Qatar FDI, central bank deposits, development assistance to select case countries, 2015–2020. *Sources*: American Enterprise Institute, fDi Markets.

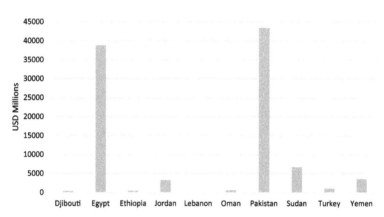

FIGURE 4.8 Saudi FDI, central bank deposits, development assistance to select case countries, 2015–2020. *Sources*: American Enterprise Institute, fDi Markets.

represents a different trend in preference in UAE intervention in the case countries. Egypt figures prominently after the Arab Spring and counter-revolution in 2013, but Oman and Pakistan have more recently been recipients of this economic statecraft. The shift might be a useful warning of the transitory nature of Gulf intervention, how flows can accelerate and then decline within a year's time.

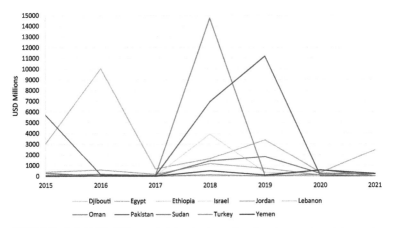

FIGURE 4.9 UAE FDI, central bank deposits, development assistance to select case countries, 2015–2021. *Sources*: American Enterprise Institute, fDi Markets.

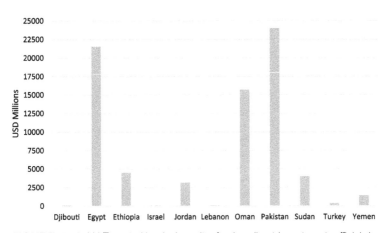

FIGURE 4.10 UAE central bank deposits, foreign direct investment, official development aid, and oil and gas in-kind assistance, 2015–2020 (in USS millions). *Sources*: American Enterprise Institute, fDi Markets.

Conclusions

Pakistan and Oman have needed external support and have in some ways avoided major economic reforms and governance reforms with this support. Despite tensions and very real security dilemmas, Oman and Pakistan relied upon China and the Gulf states as sources of authoritarian capital. These capital injections have tended to strengthen limited sectors of the Pakistani and Omani economies—energy, ports, infrastructure, but not necessarily major job creation or acceleration of technology transfer or upskilling of the labor force. In conjunction with heavy military assistance from the US since 2001 in Pakistan and a general lack of US interest in governance reform in the Gulf, the outcomes of these political economies are very clear. The design of development objectives has been complicated with security concerns, long-standing political alliances, and driven by the state(s) rather than business needs or market considerations. Access to capital similarly is funneled through these political relationships, which has pointed Oman and Pakistan toward China, and toward their Gulf partners.

5 TOO LITTLE, TOO LATE: DEVELOPMENT IN CRISIS — CASE STUDIES OF SUDAN AND YEMEN

In December 2021, Saudi and Emirati warplanes attacked a Houthi weapons depot in a sports stadium in Sanaa, Yemen's capital (France 24, 2021). Saudi and Emirati military engagement in Yemen continues more than six years after the Houthis overthrew the government of Yemen in late 2014 and the Gulf intervention began in March 2015, as both the UAE and Saudi Arabia engaged to restore the government, with UN Security Council resolution 2216 as backing (Security Council, 2015). At the same time in December 2021, protestors in Sudan were calling for the return to civilian rule, after a military coup on October 25, 2021 (News Wires, 2021). The transitional civilian rule that successfully overthrew Omar al Bashir, Sudan's despotic leader of thirty years in the spring of 2019, descended back to authoritarian control within three years, with the external support in some cases of Saudi Arabia and the United Arab Emirates (Zunes, 2021). Both of these conflicts have demonstrated the willingness of the Gulf Arab states to intervene to support regional governments. In both cases, the governments they support are ones in crisis, struggling for legitimacy and against insurgency and/or revolution.

Sudan and Yemen are fragile states by definition and prone to external influence and internal limits of state capacity. They are poor public service providers, deficient job creators, and liabilities to their neighbors, particularly as they can be a haven for terrorist organizations. For the

Gulf states, there are two decision points: first, whether to intervene to change the outcome of a leadership struggle, and second, to try and recommend or impose a different economic model. In both decision points to intervene, the justification is a return on that action and investment, what is best for the security and economic interests of the Gulf state itself. In this respect, the transfer and imposition of a development model may not have a primary goal of economic growth and transformation of the recipient state. Those benefits are secondary.

Throughout this book, cases of Gulf financial aid and intervention have shown why states are motivated to direct capital and support, and how they may choose to do so. In each case, development, as an objective, is overlaid with domestic economic, security, and political considerations. In this sense, what the Gulf states do is no different than other global development state actors. It is how the Gulf states intervene that is often different; sometimes less institutionalized, more personalistic, and even more direct and less bureaucratic. The outcomes, however, are evaluated by national standards, or more precisely, by the criteria of the leadership directly. Quite simply, the measuring stick is different.

Interventions by the United States and European Union member states are often separated, with security and military engagements evaluated apart from foreign aid budgets and humanitarian relief operations. China's deployment of economic tools abroad is also directly correlated to national economic goals at home, as its own domestic bank system increasingly relies on lending to sovereigns abroad to support its banks' asset balance sheets. (Horn et al., 2019). In each instance, this is economic statecraft at work.

The Gulf states' deployment of aid and financial intervention in extreme cases, as we see in Yemen and Sudan, is important because it lays bare how external actors measure and evaluate their own rationale for getting involved. The Gulf states tend to have a very realist and self-interested rationale for their economic interventions, whether aid or investment. For other states, especially the United States and its European partners, there can also be a different sense of obligation and of a real effort at transformation of the recipient political economy. These are ideas and ways of thinking about both development as an objective and intervention as mechanisms to achieve social, political, and economic change.

Take, for example, US foreign aid to Afghanistan since 2001, and its spectacular collapse in 2021. The security objective to defeat the Taliban and destroy a haven for extremists responsible for the September 11, 2001 attacks on the United States was the primary rationale for military intervention. But what came afterwards was a belief that Afghanistan could not only be changed, but changed in the model of American ideals of democracy and gender equality. The concentration of aid to women and girls revolutionized global humanitarian efforts to see gender equality as means to achieve economic growth. USAID calls this "mainstreaming gender" into its country aid strategy (USAID, 2022). A cultural norm became an economic argument, and in some instances, a justification of military engagement. That the United States was willing to spend enormous amounts of capital ($2.31 trillion, estimated by Brown University's Watson Institute) and the lives of its soldiers on this effort, only to abandon it two decades later and see a complete reversal to Taliban rule (Watson Institute, 2021). The US gave up hope of changing Afghanistan and blamed its government (and its people) for a failure to see the value in what the American intervention had tried to achieve (Holland & Bose, 2021). For the Gulf states, they too may abandon an aid partner or client, but they do not generally do so because they see their efforts at transformation have failed. They will see instead a threat diminished or a more pressing challenge deserving their money and attention elsewhere.

In this sense, the Saudi and Emirati interventions in Yemen since 2015 should be understood as reactions to a direct security threat on the Arabian Peninsula. Neither is interested in remaking or nation-building in Yemen. And in many ways, neither the UAE nor Saudi Arabia is interested in combining their efforts on behalf of Yemenis, but rather securing discrete interests in different territorial jurisdictions within Yemen, united or separate. The intervention in Yemen has been costly reputationally for both Saudi Arabia and the United Arab Emirates. Future aid and investment might be contingent on a calculation of value for that effort, when so little of the humanitarian aid is recognized internationally. From the Saudi perspective, failures in the military campaign overshadow the good work done in humanitarian aid. According to the Yemen Data Project, between 2015 and 2019, over 17,000 civilians were victims of Saudi coalition air attacks (Yemen Data Project, 2019).

In Sudan, the opportunity to intervene has been a low-hanging fruit, a low-cost and potentially high-yield maneuver with little competition or protest from other international actors. And the potential benefit of influence in Sudan can extend beyond the Horn of Africa and traditional linkages of food security or mining opportunity. The Abraham Accords are one example of leveraging financial support for a broader regional security and diplomatic initiative, as Sudan followed Bahrain and the United Arab Emirates in normalizing ties with Israel in 2020.

Not all Gulf states try these financial interventions, certainly even fewer flex their military assets. Kuwait, Oman, and Bahrain rarely do. Oman has been a source of diplomatic intervention in the Yemen conflict based on territorial necessity, but also out of concern for the precedent of Saudi and Emirati military engagement on the Arabian Peninsula. Qatar has been more trepidatious in its efforts in Yemen and Sudan, and to a small degree also in support of Oman. Largely less able or willing to use military force, Qatar does offer financial support. Although in Yemen, Qatar's offers of security assistance were ultimately unwelcome by the Saudi-led coalition (Reuters, 2017b).

These two cases, Sudan and Yemen, represent more of the extreme development challenge. But they also represent for the Gulf states a different way of thinking and engaging states in crisis. It is a different way of thinking about using financial and military intervention to achieve development objectives altogether. In Sudan and in Yemen, it is primarily the Gulf states, not China, the United States, or European Union member states that are leading negotiations for peace and spending their own blood and treasure in stabilization, and ultimately, growth incentives. And for that reason alone, trying to understand how and why the Gulf states might engage within their own region with their own financial resources presents a window into the logic of their individual modes of economic statecraft. For Saudi Arabia and the UAE, when they are the leaders what do they do?

To juxtapose Gulf financial aid and intervention in extreme cases of political crisis and conflict against Western interventions, consider the prior relationship Gulf leaders enjoyed over the thirty-year tenure of both former dictators in Yemen and Sudan. Omar al Bashir was very welcome in Abu Dhabi, often seen as a VIP guest at the Formula One races over the years. In fact, between January 2017 and March 2018, the UAE channeled a total $7.6 billion in the form of support to Sudan's central bank, in private investments and investments through the Abu Dhabi Fund for Development, all before al Bashir was forced from power (Abdelaziz et al., 2019). And Ali Abdullah Saleh was the recipient of significant Saudi support for decades, and even after his about face turn to partner with the Houthis, Saudi and Emirati leadership acknowledged his usefulness as a political actor (Patrick, 2017). The rush to intervene was not to hurry out the failed leaders of the past and support a transformation to a more open political order, but to ensure that the relationship continued and possibly improved in any new political environment. This is the difference of Gulf financial aid and intervention in the sense that it is not ideologically driven, or even necessarily results or development outcome driven. It is relationship driven. The assumption is that the relationship from the side of Gulf leadership is unwavering, which is a statement of confidence in their own political longevity. On the other hand, recipient states and rival political factions also understand the fungibility of Gulf support and may adopt strategies to secure Gulf aid and investment commitments in return for policy or personnel choices.

Gulf Financial Aid and Investment Interventions in Sudan

Alex de Waal describes the Gulf and Sudanese political economies as linked and similar in striking ways, as competitive political marketplaces. Sudan's political economy is also heavily reliant on oil revenues, in what de Waal calls a "rentier crony capitalist system" (de Waal, 2019). Oil revenues in the period from 1999–2011 (before South Sudan independence) helped generate new industries and businesses, as well as sustain a centralized government of "kleptocracy," as de Waal defines it. The lead up to the separation of South Sudan and then the removal of Omar al Bashir, was the failure of the political system to continue to generate rents from natural resource revenue to draw to the center and then redistribute. The whole system seems to have fallen apart from the end of the ability to share the material benefits of the oil boom, which created jobs, construction, and the proliferation of other consumer commodities. Sudan's precariousness is in some ways a similar model of Gulf political economies, but also a warning of the weakness of the political center when the revenue source is either severed in ownership or sovereignty (as what happened in South Sudan) or no longer in demand (as what may come to oil producers in the energy transition). Sudan's political economy has also been highly militarized, such that the provision of security services became a source of resource revenue for the government. Sudan's willingness, both under al Bashir and in the aftermath of the political transition from 2019, to rent military personnel to Gulf states for use in Yemen, as an expeditionary and mercenary force is evidence of the poor state of dependable fiscal revenue and the willingness of a range of political actors to use the military as a negotiating tool with Gulf benefactors. In 2019, Sudan reduced the number of active military personnel for hire in Yemen from 15,000 to 5,000, but nonetheless maintained the provision of service (Abdelaziz, 2019).

The hollowing out of the state, from its military conscripts to state land use, is symbolic of the fragility of Sudan, but also of the way that recipient states might tailor their own assets to attract Gulf support. There is a long tradition of trade and investment through agricultural leases and land sales from Sudan to the Gulf states. Food security is a general way of thinking and justifying political and economic ties from the Gulf to the Horn of Africa. Scholars like Christian Henderson have argued that the discourse on food security may shield some of the profit motive of large agribusiness in the Gulf without really guaranteeing high nutrition food supply for the Gulf states. Much of the land reclamation that has occurred in both Egypt and Sudan by Gulf states purchasing or leasing land direct from governments has gone to supply large agribusinesses like Americana and other firms that supply large commercial food chains for French fries and alfalfa for livestock (Rouchdy & Hamdy, 2017, pp. 127–140). Eckart Woertz has argued that the Gulf states have now shifted a focus on food security as an availability problem to a supply chain management problem, as past approaches to using agricultural production by farmland proxy have failed (Woertz, 2020, pp. 757–760). Farmland investments in Sudan and other locations have not generated meaningful quantities to Gulf countries' food imports.

Nevertheless, the Gulf states have proved an important source of incoming capital and investment for Sudan, especially as other sources have been deterred by political instability and sanctions. The raw data is probably most illustrative of the problem Sudan has faced in attracting investment over the last two decades.

Four sending countries/regional group total over $100 million over the course of 2003–2021, but only one of those sending countries/regional group was a consistent source of capital investment over the

TABLE 5.1 *Foreign direct investment to Sudan from select countries, 2003–2021 (in US$ millions)*

	Capital Investment									
Year	Bahrain	China	European Union	Kuwait	Oman	Qatar	Saudi Arabia	United Arab Emirates	United Kingdom	United States
2003	0.00	0.00	0.00	0.00	0.00	0.00	63.40	15.00	0.00	0.00
2004	0.00	45.70	0.00	0.00	0.00	0.00	0.00	0.00	0.00	0.00
2005	0.00	0.00	0.00	0.00	0.00	0.00	0.00	203.00	0.00	0.00
2006	0.00	0.00	0.00	11.00	0.00	129.80	28.30	17.80	0.00	0.00
2007	0.00	0.00	0.00	0.00	0.00	0.00	0.00	0.00	0.00	0.00
2008	0.00	0.00	22.20	7.50	0.00	904.20	0.00	300.00	0.00	0.00
2009	0.00	1735.70	0.00	0.00	0.00	11.00	11.00	0.00	0.00	0.00
2010	0.00	0.00	1652.00	0.00	0.00	0.00	0.00	0.00	0.00	0.00
2011	0.00	0.00	0.00	0.00	0.00	0.00	11.00	9.50	0.00	0.00
2012	0.00	7.50	0.00	0.00	0.00	0.00	0.00	48.70	0.00	0.00
2013	0.00	0.00	0.00	0.00	0.00	9.50	0.00	49.90	0.00	0.00
2014	0.00	0.00	0.00	0.00	0.00	0.00	0.00	0.00	0.00	0.00

TABLE 5.1 *(Continued)*

						Capital Investment					
Year	Bahrain	China	European Union	Kuwait	Oman	Qatar	Saudi Arabia	United Arab Emirates	United Kingdom	United States
2015	0.00	0.00	0.00	94.40	0.00	0.00	10.50	100.20	0.00	0.00
2016	0.00	0.00	0.00	0.00	0.00	0.00	0.00	21.60	0.00	0.00
2017	0.00	0.00	0.00	0.00	0.00	0.00	0.00	0.00	0.00	0.00
2018	0.00	0.00	0.00	0.00	0.00	0.00	0.00	23.80	0.00	0.00
2019	0.00	0.00	0.00	2.00	0.00	0.00	0.00	0.00	0.00	0.00
2020	0.00	94.40	0.00	0.00	0.00	0.00	0.00	225.00	0.00	0.00
2021	0.00	0.00	0.00	0.00	0.00	0.00	0.00	10.50	0.00	0.00
Total	0.00	1883.30	1674.20	114.90	0.00	1054.50	124.20	1025.00	0.00	0.00

Sources: American Enterprise Institute, fDi Markets.

entire period: the United Arab Emirates. China and the European Union are also important sources of investment to Sudan, but their engagement has been limited really to the period between 2009 and 2010. Qatar was active as a source of investment between 2006 and 2009, with one major placement in 2008.

When we look at the specific firms engaged in Sudan from the UAE over the course of 2003–2021, certain sectors and activities stand out. One is IHC, International Holding Company, which was previously known as International Fish Farming Company (Asmak) formed in 2008 and grew as a land and agricultural holding firm to include a series of acquisitions in other professional services (sports) and real estate holdings (International Holding Company, n.d.). The chairman is Sheikh Tahnoon bin Zayed al Nayhan, a member of the Abu Dhabi ruling family and also national security advisor. IHC has invested in Sudan as recently as October 2020, with a $225 million placement in the commercial agriculture sector. Other significant recent placements include bank sector investments, namely from the Bank of Khartoum, which is a subsidiary of Dubai Islamic Bank since 2005. Dubai Islamic Bank is a publicly listed bank on the Dubai stock exchange, but just over 27 percent of the company is owned by the Investment Corporation of Dubai, which is fully owned by the Government of Dubai as an investment vehicle or sovereign fund (Dubai Islamic Bank, 2021).

These are examples of investments that are technically private entities, but are under some form of government-related ownership or management. These are also sectors which relate to security concerns, financial or food security. Other projects of interest include a September 2021 investment by Emirates Stallions Group, which is a subsidiary of the previously mentioned IHC, for $65 million as a real estate venture in Sudan. Similarly, the large Qatari investment into Sudan in 2008 of roughly $900 million from Barwa real estate and construction, a locally listed firm with 45 percent of its shares owned by the government's Qatar Investment Authority, the sovereign wealth fund (BARWA, 2021).

Sudan has been an easy target for large Gulf state-owned investment vehicles, predominantly parts of sovereign wealth funds or assets controlled by governments. The investments are in sectors like construction, banking or holding companies, firms that are not interested in local franchises or technology transfer or training capacity. These are vehicles for the projection of state power and interests and influence locally.

In aid disbursements, we see another pattern of Gulf economic statecraft at work. Official development assistance to Sudan has not flowed in a consistent way from the Gulf over the past twenty years. There have been moments of increased support, in times of crisis, and times of zero support. Again, the pattern of participation in aid support among the Gulf states tends to vary, as vying for support from Qatar versus the UAE or Saudi Arabia has defined a lot of the aid relationships of the Gulf and its immediate sphere of influence across the Horn and Levant. As Annette Weber (currently the EU Special Representative for the Horn of Africa) wrote as an analyst in late 2019, the greatest challenge facing Sudan is its economic management:

> Its greatest challenge is its weak economy. At present, the country is largely dependent on oil from South Sudan and injections of capital from the Gulf States. Prime Minister Hamdok has requested eight billion US dollars to support the strategy he intends to pursue over the next two years and two billion US dollars in foreign reserve deposits. His plans also require debt relief and access to international financial institutions. Moreover, it is important he initiates a rapid diversification of the economy and makes greater efforts to break up the mafia-like entanglements of the old regime. Expanding agriculture, promoting investment and building industry are just as necessary as the return of the well-trained Sudanese people needed to rebuild Sudan's ailing economy.
>
> **WEBER**, 2019, p. 5

What Weber and other Sudan analysts understood very well in 2019 was that the design of the economy had not changed, despite the major upheaval politically in removing a dictator and sharing power among a very entrenched and problematic military elite. Patterns of economic management and ideas about how best to grow have not changed. Moreover, the primary sources of external support have only narrowed to deepen dependency on the Gulf and to see Western states and financial institutions as obstacles and mechanisms to debt relief, not necessarily as potential investors or incubators of economic change. Most challenging is an unresolved issue of revenue-sharing of oil resources and post-federalist and separatist politics. This for the Gulf states, especially the UAE, is a sensitive topic and not one for which they are in a position to offer creative solutions.

The US position in 2019 did indeed center on debt management, along with cash and food support, and there was little appetite for further political or economic intervention. In August 2021, USAID Administrator Samantha Power lauded that the United States is the single largest humanitarian donor to Sudan, providing nearly $377 million since the beginning of fiscal year 2021 (USAID Office of Press Relations, 2021). Yet, by October 2021, Congress was obligated to halt US aid to Sudan as the military overtook the civilian coalition government in a counter-coup (Walsh, 2021). In June 2021, the US Treasury Department announced support for the settlement of $1.4 billion in Sudan's arrears to the International Monetary Fund, facilitating a way for a new support facility (US Department of the Treasury, 2021).

Interestingly, the announced support in terms of investment flows from the Gulf in 2019 had not met expectations by the end of 2021. The lack of access to IMF support or other donors closed off after the military coup in October 2021, pushing Sudan back to its Gulf supporters (Marks, 2021). But the promises of the previous two years also remained unmet. According to the UN and US government assessments, the on-going conflict and displacement of people impedes basic access to services, food, and protection. Sudan also experienced its worst flooding in more than 100 years in 2020. The UN estimates that 14.3 million people will need humanitarian assistance in Sudan in 2022 (USAID, 2021b). And unfortunately, three years after its successful turn to representative government, Sudan is outside of many forms of financial aid and assistance channels.

Over the last few years, Gulf humanitarian aid has been an important source of support to Sudan as well. The Abu Dhabi Fund for Development is one important source, along with direct cash deposits. But the volatility especially between 2019, at the beginning of Sudan's transition, to 2020 with the Covid-19 pandemic and less optimism of the new government underway, speak to the vulnerability of large swings in flows. Figure 5.1 also demonstrates the priority of Sudan among the top three destinations of Gulf aid and investment, behind Pakistan and Egypt in 2019.

In Saudi Arabia, we also see a dedicated commitment of aid and investment to Sudan, but it is secondary or tertiary to support going to Pakistan, Egypt, Yemen, and Jordan (in that order) between 2015 and 2020 (Figure 5.2). For Qatar, aid to Yemen and Sudan is inconsequential compared to other core recipients, especially Pakistan. Figure 5.3 gives a

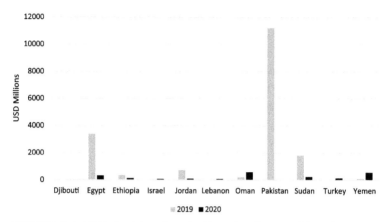

FIGURE 5.1 UAE direct investment, aid, and cash support to select countries, 2019–2020. *Sources*: American Enterprise Institute, fDi Markets.

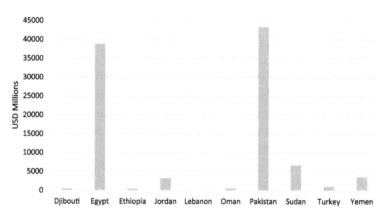

FIGURE 5.2 Saudi direct cash support, direct investment, and official development assistance to select countries, 2015–2020 (in US$ millions). *Sources*: American Enterprise Institute, fDi Markets, national sources.

look at overall official development assistance, direct cash support and foreign direct investment in 2019-2020 as a sample year and the dominance of Pakistan is revealing a shared Gulf priority, even over the humanitarian catastrophe in Yemen and the year of tremendous upheaval in Sudan.

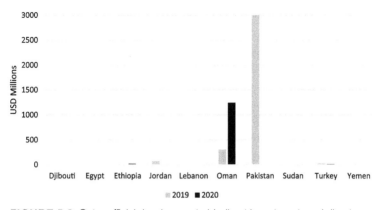

FIGURE 5.3 Qatar official development aid, direct investment, and direct support to select countries, 2019–2020 (in US$ millions). *Sources*: American Enterprise Institute, fDi Markets, national sources.

A Breakthrough in Regional Investment Flows? Not for Now

In this same period, between 2019 and 2020, something else of significance occurred in Gulf-Sudanese relations which may be more of an indicator of support and use of leverage after the financial commitments to Sudan in 2019. The normalization of ties between Israel and the United Arab Emirates and Bahrain signed in fall 2020 then led to a series of diplomatic openings for Israel with other Arab states, including Sudan and Morocco. The Trump Administration in the United States lauded the Abraham Accords as an opportunity specifically for regional financial integration and direct investment. For Israel and the United Arab Emirates, this has indeed heralded a series of mostly state-owned investment commitments from the UAE to Israel, including an investment in Israel's Eastern Mediterranean gas fields, a major pipeline through the Sinai, and in technology and security firms. For Sudan, this has meant very little in terms of incoming investment or improved trade ties with Israel.

Normalization between Israel and Bahrain and the United Arab Emirates, the Abraham Accords were meant to open the gates of tourism, trade, and investment flows (Young, 2021a). Early estimates of the potential of increased trade and investment were exuberant, with predicted trade flows to reach $4 billion per year within three years

(Reuters, 2020). More than 50,000 Israelis flocked to Dubai over the New Year's holiday in early 2021 (Holleis, 2021). In March 2021, the UAE announced plans for a $10 billion fund to invest in and alongside Israel in "strategic sectors" in the Israeli economy, including manufacturing, energy, and health care (WAM, 2021). The real impact of the Abraham Accords in terms of new capital investment flows at its outset are modest and more generous flowing from the UAE to Israel; flows into Bahrain have been even slower to materialize and nothing to Sudan.

According to data from fDi Markets, between September 2020 and the end of March 2021, there were just five deals as a source of capital investment in the UAE from Israeli firms. In total, the capital investment was less than $25 million and created about 120 jobs in the UAE. The firms are in health care (Hadassah Medical Center and Aviv Scientific), a consulting firm that will establish an industrial zone incubator, a diamond firm, and an AI technology company that provides traffic solutions (Spencer, 2020).

In comparison, UAE-based capital investment in Israel between September 2020 and March 2021 was more than three times as much, at about $80 million, but in just three placements. The largest reported investment in Israel was from Group42, an AI firm that is itself funded by the UAE sovereign wealth fund Mubadala and Silver Lake, a California-based technology investment firm. The other investments were by Paramount Group, an aerospace and defense firm headquartered in Abu Dhabi now with a location in Israel, and an investment from Habtoor Group, a UAE conglomerate. These are all investments that are resistant to domestic pressure to disengage from Israel, as long as the government continues to stand behind normalization. They are also investments that are safe from international pressures of divestment, as they are largely state-related entities or private firms with consolidated leadership and ownership.

The relationship between the UAE and Israel is still in the early stages. Israel is keen to preserve the partnership and the visit by the foreign minister is proof of its strategic importance. The UAE is the top destination in the Middle East for greenfield foreign direct investment projects, accounting for 32 percent of projects in the region. In dollar amounts, the UAE attracted $9 billion in greenfield capital investment in 2020, while Israel attracted just $1.9 billion, according to the FDI 2021 report on global greenfield investment. Israel's technology advantage and start-up culture is a draw for the Emirates, but those relationships are also built on trust and knowledge communities. Investing in people-to-people ties between the Gulf and Israel will do a lot to meet shared goals of investment and growth.

Gulf Financial Aid and Investment in Yemen

Assessing the role of GCC member states in driving economic aid and investment in Yemen is a complicated task. Yemen shares a border with Saudi Arabia and Oman, has long-standing trade links, employment and family networks throughout the Arabian Peninsula. Yemen is also an historical empire, the site of an imamate and claim to a civilization that other Gulf states do not share, with the exception of the Omanis, who also claim a past empire with territories in Asia and the coast of East Africa. The current socioeconomic position of Yemen is of course a different situation, one rife with internal conflict, the threat of intervention by external powers, and overwhelming poverty and lack of resources. The Gulf states are parties to conflict in Yemen, actively sending warplanes and funding fighters and militias and political organizations. And sometimes their support goes to different factions and fuels internal feuds. Yet, Saudi Arabia remains Yemen's most important source of direct humanitarian aid and has long been a driving source of foreign currency and income through remittances of Yemeni workers in the kingdom. The United Arab Emirates is actively engaged in development work in Yemen, centered in the South of Yemen and in discrete areas of interest, including the strategically located island of Socotra. Oman has been an active diplomatic force in the Yemen, hosting different political factions and facilitating dialogue.

Most of all, Yemen is a threat to the GCC states in the liability of a population at its borders that lives a completely different standard of health, education, and economic opportunity and presents itself as a potential haven for terrorism and disorder. That disorder is most visible in the rise of the Houthi movement, a domestic constituency, but one that has actively and successfully received external financial and military support from Iran. For Saudi Arabia and the United Arab Emirates, they fear the rise of a Hezbollah-like organization that receives material and ideological support from Iran and uses terrorism to achieve its goals. With the attack on three fuel tankers with three fatalities near the Abu

Dhabi airport in January 2022, the Houthis seem to have achieved a goal of directing a major security threat to the Gulf states (Faucon & Nissenbaum, 2022). Persistent Houthi drone and projectile attacks on Saudi territory have received less attention during the war, but are a demonstration of the group's intensifying capacity and willingness to target civilian infrastructure (Jones et al., 2021). Since January 2018, according to Saudi military chief Al Malki, the Houthis have launched 430 ballistic missiles and 850 drones toward Saudi Arabia (Reuters, 2021a).

According to the United Nations and UNICEF operations in Yemen, more than six years into the conflict, Yemen is the world's worst humanitarian crisis. In total, 20.7 million people, just over 70 percent of the population, are in need of humanitarian assistance. The war has created a series of problems in access to aid and care, but environmental problems and the Covid-19 pandemic have intensified the public health crisis and left four million people internally displaced. Yemenis have suffered considerably, but the country is also host to a large number of refugees from the Horn of Africa. UNICEF estimates as many as 138,000 migrants and 177,000 refugees and asylum-seekers are in Yemen, and 90 percent of them are from Ethiopia. Ethiopia is of course another case country of this study and example of the intersection of Gulf economics and politics in a widening sphere of influence, some with disastrous consequences for the people between the regions (UNICEF, 2021).

Saudi Arabia shares over 1,100 miles of border with Yemen; the kingdom is sensitive to the prospect that political, economic, or social unrest in Yemen will reverberate across a border that in many locations is lightly patrolled. Saudi Arabia has been an investor and provider of infrastructure development across Yemen. More informally, Saudi Arabia has long used transfers of cash and incentives to Yemeni government officials, political figures, and tribal leaders. In March 2015, Saudi Arabia, leading a coalition of Arab countries, entered Yemen's war in an effort to achieve three core goals: to restore President Hadi and the Yemeni internationally recognized government; to counter and cut Iran's support for the Houthis and its influence in Yemen; and to secure the southern border from incursions and missile attacks.

The cost of lives in Yemen's humanitarian disaster is incalculable, but the cost of waging war in Yemen for external parties has also been high in war machinery and personnel. The social science research on civil wars demonstrates that the economic cost of conflicts tends to multiply, with effects in the domestic economy and toward neighboring states. Civil wars are regional growth decelerators. Stefano Costalli, Costantino Pischedda, and Luigi Moretti (2017) show that civil wars have the effect of reducing average annual per capita GDP growth by about 1.5 percent during conflict and continuing in the aftermath. It is not just that war devastates economies, but civil wars tend to devastate possibilities for economic recovery for a long time. There is an expectation that the Gulf states, specifically the UAE and Saudi Arabia, will lead as funders and agents of post-conflict reconstruction in Yemen. The lack of political, economic, and military coordination between Saudi Arabia and the UAE has been a constant impediment to the military campaign and to unity within the opposition to the Houthi movement.

Throughout the war between 2015 and 2022, the blockade of ports and control over air access and highways has made institutional apparatus to coordinate aid and humanitarian relief. The King Salman Humanitarian Aid and Relief Centre is a Saudi initiative, but there is no parallel UAE center, nor is there evidence of capacity for large-scale aid delivery and reconstruction. For that reason, the reconstruction of Yemen will rely on regional funding and delivery capacity but with an overarching international mandate and delivery system. The structure of Yemen's economy weakens its chances of recovery and broadens its regional economic fallout in several ways. Yemen's economy is heavily dependent on oil exports and food imports. According to a World Bank study on the economics of post-conflict reconstruction in the Middle East and North Africa, for the last thirty years, Yemen has relied on oil for more than a third of its gross domestic product ($31 billion in 2010), half of its government revenue, and 90 percent of its exports (MENA Economic Monitor, 2017). During the oil boom between 2003 and 2014, high oil revenues allowed the central government of Yemen to provide employment in the public sector and make some infrastructure investment. Yemen's economy grew at an average annual rate of 3.8 percent between 1990 and 2010. The oil revenue growth in the upcycle of 2021–2022 is not reliable and subject to renewed divisions of authority within Yemen and increasing pressure to form an independent region in the South.

Even with new aid commitments, Yemen will grapple with the legacy of conflict and the problem of re-establishing trust. The long-standing grievances of inequality of access to resources will be a key obstacle in reconstruction. Moreover, the demographics of Yemen reinforce the vulnerabilities of the local economy. According to a study by the World Bank, United Nations, Islamic Development Bank, and European Union, there is a strong link between youth and work in the informal sector: in Yemen, 21.9 percent of employed people are between the ages of 15 and 24, and 97.2 percent of them work in the informal sector (MENA Economic Monitor, 2017). Young people are exposed to higher levels of vulnerability than older workers. The demographic challenge of post-conflict reconstruction in Yemen is potentially an area for policy adaptation, as the Gulf states also need to create policy prescriptions to boost youth employment. For the Gulf Arab states, the risk of a young, unemployed, fractionalized society at its border with increasing capacity for sophisticated weaponry, and little access to public health services or education, is unacceptable. But the price of transforming that society is also exceedingly high, and a model of how to do so, seemingly out of reach.

Saudi aid and economic development initiatives since the start of the conflict in 2015 have evolved in style and format, adopting frameworks of the United Nation's Sustainable Development Goals (SDGs). Saudi efforts to publicize their development and aid work in Yemen have led to a kind of institutionalization of the government's aid agencies. For example, the Saudi Development and Reconstruction Program in Yemen (SDPRY) is the key body for government aid and development grants in Yemen. It has partnered with the Islamic Development Bank to design a curriculum for executive management programs in development, as the deployment of aid has become a burgeoning third sector for Saudi nationals entering the development field (Islamic Development Bank, 2021b). The SDPRY has a number of programs operating in Yemen for local community development, many that target women entrepreneurs, green initiatives in cities, new construction of schools (including a "talented and gifted program" roll-out), and sanitation programs. An example of the literature promoting the programs in Marib for women is called "The Economic Experiment," which is emblematic of much of the programming (Figure 5.4). It is experimental, both in the context of operations in Yemen and from the donor, which is also developing its own national priorities for women in the workforce.

For the UAE, the formation of the Ministry for Foreign Affairs and International Cooperation has also taken on Yemen as a core recipient of government aid programs, along with an expansion of efforts in a wider geography in East Africa, in North Africa, and across the Middle East. The

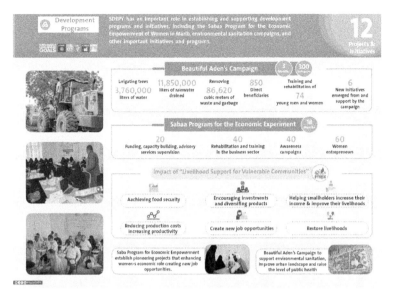

FIGURE 5.4 Saudi Development and Reconstruction Program for Yemen (SDRPY), "Sabaa Program for Economic Empowerment of Women in Marib." *Source*: Saudi Development and Reconstruction Program for Yemen.

efforts of the international cooperation portfolio include traditional development assistance, but also economic cooperation, which is a catch-all consideration of trade and foreign direct investment incentive packages.

Overall, official development assistance from the GCC states to Yemen has been led by Saudi Arabia and the United Arab Emirates, both historically since 2003 and since the start (or entry of Gulf external actors) of the latest civil war in 2015. But there is little in the form of direct investment in Yemen, from the Gulf states or from Western investors or China. And since 2015, capital inflows have nearly completely dried up. What we find instead are some one-off projects in the early to mid-2000s in particular, that are not repeated.

So, while the Gulf states, the UAE and Saudi Arabia more specifically, have accepted a role in the humanitarian situation in Yemen and a responsibility to provide assistance and to reconstruct its economy after the war, there is a long history of weak investment and aid dependency. And the new history is one of development design on the go, literally planning and delivering development aid in the midst of an on-going war. The post-war reconstruction will more likely follow the pre-war aid

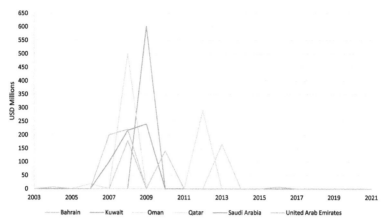

FIGURE 5.5 GCC official development assistance to Yemen, 2003–2021. *Sources*: American Enterprise Institute, national sources.

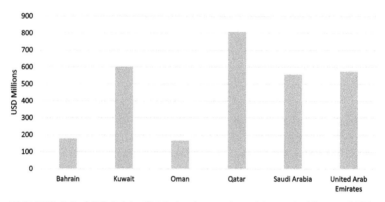

FIGURE 5.6 GCC total official development assistance to Yemen, 2003–2021. *Sources*: American Enterprise Institute, national sources.

and investment trajectory, one that is relatively sporadic. As Ginny Hill argues in her authoritative account of Yemen's political disorder:

> The failure of international mediation suggests that Yemen's wars look set to continue—possibly for many years to come; meanwhile the tasks of reconciliation and reconstruction already appear formidable. The outcome of this latest power struggle between rival groups within Yemen, and between Yemen and its Gulf neighbours, will affect the structure of the state and the future of Arabia.
>
> 2017, p. 8

TABLE 5.2 *Capital investment to Yemen, various country sources, 2003–2021 (US$ millions)*

				Capital Investment						
Year	Bahrain	China	European Union	Kuwait	Oman	Qatar	Saudi Arabia	United Arab Emirates	United Kingdom	United States
2003	0.00	10.00	0.00	0.00	0.00	0.00	0.00	0.00	125.00	0.00
2004	0.00	0.00	0.00	0.00	0.00	0.00	0.00	7.00	0.00	0.00
2005	0.00	0.00	3466.70	0.00	0.00	0.00	0.00	0.00	0.00	7.40
2006	0.00	0.00	0.00	0.00	0.00	18.60	0.00	0.00	0.00	0.00
2007	0.00	0.00	6.50	0.00	0.00	0.00	100.00	200.00	0.00	0.00
2008	178.20	0.00	415.68	0.00	0.00	500.00	216.70	220.00	0.00	0.00
2009	0.00	0.00	0.00	600.90	0.00	0.00	240.00	0.00	0.00	0.00
2010	0.00	0.00	0.00	0.00	0.00	0.00	0.00	140.00	0.00	0.00
2011	0.00	0.00	0.00	0.00	0.00	0.00	0.00	0.00	0.00	0.00
2012	0.00	0.00	0.00	0.00	0.00	289.00	0.00	0.00	0.00	0.00
2013	0.00	0.00	0.00	0.00	165.60	0.00	0.00	0.00	0.00	0.00
2014	0.00	121.30	19.90	0.00	0.00	0.00	0.00	0.00	0.00	121.30
2015	0.00	0.00	0.00	0.00	0.00	0.00	0.00	0.00	0.00	0.00

TABLE 5.2 (Continud).

						Capital Investment						
Year	Bahrain	China	European Union	Kuwait	Oman	Qatar	Saudi Arabia	United Arab Emirates	United Kingdom	United States
2016	0.00	0.00	0.00	0.00	0.00	0.00	0.00	6.90	0.00	0.00
2017	0.00	0.00	0.00	0.00	0.00	0.00	0.00	0.00	0.00	0.00
2018	0.00	0.00	0.00	0.00	0.00	0.00	0.00	0.00	0.00	0.00
2019	0.00	0.00	0.00	0.00	0.00	0.00	0.00	0.00	0.00	0.00
2020	0.00	0.00	0.00	0.00	0.00	0.00	0.00	0.00	0.00	0.00
2021	0.00	0.00	0.00	0.00	0.00	0.00	0.00	0.00	0.00	0.00
Total	178.20	131.30	3908.78	600.90	165.60	807.60	556.70	573.90	125.00	128.70

Sources: American Enterprise Institute, fDi Markets.

What Hill describes is a process not just of state-making and state disintegration in Yemen, but of the formation and structuring of a regional dynamic on the Arabian Peninsula, which is becoming a pattern of intervention, the use of economic tools of statecraft combined with military force. For the Gulf states, these are sometimes first efforts at foreign intervention of this kind. The lessons learned will be enormous, but the patterns of engagement are already in action across a widening sphere of influence.

CONCLUSION

The New Geopolitics of Energy and the Role of the Gulf State Development Actors

The concluding chapter seeks to square the circle, acknowledging the current power and resources deployed from the Gulf and the clear need for new sources of finance for development, especially in renewable energy across the Middle East and Horn of Africa. For governments interested in the promotion of rules-based economies and liberal markets, there might be ways to combine development resources and private capital to work as an alternative to state-led solutions, or at least work in partnership with them. For those governments seeking aid and financial support from the Gulf, there are reasons to proceed with caution and to try and create leverage on the ground, in promoting skilled job training and worker benefits to build local capacity.

But there is no way around the reality that the Gulf states are increasingly the most important sources of investment and financial intervention in a widening sphere of influence across the Middle East and Horn of Africa. Their financial interventions rival the aid and investment capacity of much larger states, and those with much longer track records in humanitarian assistance, as well as their own industrialization journeys. A valid question becomes, "So what?" Is there a reason to believe that Western state actors and sources of capital, or even China and its state-led growth model, are better suited than the Gulf states to engage their own region? Are the outcomes that we have seen from Western investment different in measurable ways? How does a Gulf preference for investing in certain sectors via state entities funnel or limit economic growth or mobility in the recipient country?

What this book has shown is that there are patterns to Gulf, especially Saudi and Emirati, aid and investment strategies in recipient case countries. There is also tremendous volatility over time and in volume. Gulf economic statecraft is not more or less political than the actions of other states. It is, if anything, more exacting and precise, at least in the outcomes Gulf states want to achieve. Institutionally, their foreign policies are designed to hold a role for economic intervention, even explicitly engaging an investment arm as part of the Ministry of Foreign Affairs in the UAE. It is the anticipated or hopeful outcomes that are perhaps different for the Gulf states than how other states, Western or China, use their economic statecraft tools. As we saw in the case of Sudan, Gulf aid and investment was willing to engage Sudan both under a dictator Bashir and under a transition attempt to democracy, albeit with a heavy military presence. The politics of local rule were less important than access to local rule. In preference for sectors in investments, we see food security in line with energy projects, and a strong Gulf preference for real estate development models that parallel their own domestic designs. This is true in Gulf investment in Egypt, as it is in Ethiopia.

The likely next phase of Gulf investment and aid will be focused on renewable energy in the wider region, and there will certainly be an expectation of a return on investment and a mechanism to forward Gulf energy firms into new sectors and expertise, especially solar power. And as Jason Bordoff and Meghan O'Sullivan (2022) have argued, the expected effects in geopolitics will not necessarily be less volatile or prone to conflict as many see the effects of Middle East oil markets. A transition to more clean energy production globally will reconfigure international politics, much in the way that oil-fueled industrialization after World War II reconfigured the international system. New forms of competition are likely to play out in the developing world, and those countries that both control sources of components for new energy and those countries that have the largest need for energy imports. Those states that are traditional fossil fuel suppliers will benefit in the early market disruption as investors move away from carbon-intensive industries. Some petrostates like Saudi Arabia have a lot to gain in the interim transition period, because of their spare capacity and ability to intervene in global supply.

The larger point is that some of the Gulf states will be especially well-positioned to take advantage of the energy transition across their sphere of influence. In Bordoff and O'Sullivan's conceptualization, there are four key areas of power and influence in the new energy geopolitics: an ability to control standards in renewables from flaring technology and practices to carbon capture to nuclear energy production; access and dominance in the supply chain of minerals and inputs for solar and new energy technology; cheaper manufacturing of components; and lower cost production of fossil fuels to build a lot of those components made from petrochemicals. Saudi Arabia and the UAE are well-placed in at least three of these areas.

The Gulf as Financial Lifeline in Climate Adaptation in Middle East

The Middle East is at the center of our global energy transition and we can expect the next five to ten years to be a period of difficult transformation, but also a unique opportunity for oil and gas producers (Young, 2021b). The goal of the transition is to attempt to limit the increase of the global average temperature to below 2°C and achieve a net-zero emissions energy system by 2050. The early stage of the transition in the next five years presents a window in which the Middle East can be a bridge in terms of new technology, cleaner hydrocarbon production, and innovative change in the delivery of electricity from renewables. There is also the advantage of strong medium-term oil demand which investors are not running to meet, as capital expenditure in upstream oil and gas plummets in 2021, expected to reach less than half of its 2014 peak of $752 billion. For now, it's "Drill, baby drill," but in five to ten years, the mantra may be "Sell, baby sell" (or "We wish we had sold") as national oil companies seek to streamline some of their assets to distribute risk. Distributing risk among partners will bring some privatization to traditional oil and gas operations but will also pull producers closer to their customers (predominantly in Asia), both politically and economically.

While state-owned oil and gas businesses will reap the rewards of higher prices now, there are few expectations of major policy innovation across the Middle East, in terms of reduced domestic energy consumption and limits to extractive industries. Government targets of renewable energy production for electricity are ambitious in a few places (e.g., Djibouti aims for 100 percent renewables by 2035), but execution has been limited; the Middle East generates less than 2 percent of its electricity needs from renewable sources (excluding hydropower) and many governments heavily subsidize the cost of power (whether or not they are hydrocarbon producers) (Statista Research Department, 2020; Mohseni-Cheraghlou, 2021). Morocco stands out as a leader in using 35 percent renewable energy for its domestic energy mix (Zawya, 2021b). But this comes as a result of years of investment and collaboration with European Union efforts to incubate the sector (European Commission, n.d.). For MENA oil and gas producers, the shifts now and for the next five years are likely to concentrate on: monetization of existing resources, changing products to meet consumer preferences (whether making LNG or oil "cleaner" in its extraction, or investing in non-carbon energy carriers like green hydrogen along with improving expertise in petrochemical production), and concentrating on market share and customer relationships.

While competition for export markets will reconfigure geopolitical ties abroad, at home the Middle East will be ground zero of twenty-first-century domestic contestations over state utility service delivery, and the ability to demonstrate competence in natural resource revenue distribution. A lot can go wrong, but it will be in the interests of the United States and the key consumers of Middle East energy products in Asia and across emerging markets to invest not just in state efforts to master the production of renewable energy sources like solar and green hydrogen, but to encourage the decentralized potential of renewables in distributed solar power and independent power producers that can operate across national and even regional grid systems.

If this is indeed the next and last oil boom, there will be a period of re-fitting within national oil companies of the region to transform their businesses to include interim fuels like LNG, and to double-down on petrochemical production, while also making advances into new energy products like solar and green hydrogen for electricity generation and non-carbon energy carriers. And across the Middle East, the dominance of national oil companies will see some regional behemoths with significant advantage in access to capital, either through debt or asset sales and new investment partnerships. This interim period will also see some consistent demand for oil products particularly in aviation and maritime transport fuels, and in heavy industries for the production of cement, aluminum, and steel, for example.

However, for those countries now just beginning to consider shifting domestic electricity generation from oil- and gas-fired plants to renewables, there will be a considerable lag in access to the financing to build new plants and the process of updating grid systems and delivery of new power production. Here the United States, international financial institutions, and those Western and wealthy states driving the policy consensus toward a net-zero emissions energy system have an obligation to facilitate capital flows for the construction of renewable power infrastructure.

As a region, the Middle East will retain its share of hydrocarbon production in a market that may see reduced production in many other geographies, because of diminished investment in exploration and production, and because of a dynamic policy landscape that discourages new oil and gas extraction. With the blessing of low-cost production and generally lower CO_2 emissions associated with oil production, some Gulf producers (notably Saudi Arabia, the UAE, and Kuwait) will be able to leverage their capacity with shifting consumer preferences in cleaner sourcing (Woertz, 2021). In the gas market, the same consumer preference is already shaping a market for low carbon LNG, and gas has more runway to grow as a share in the global energy consumption mix through 2040. There will be new inequities both among oil and gas producers in the Middle East, and between those exporters and their importer neighbors in the region. We can expect new trade flows and new kinds of product demand, as demand for gasoline for internal combustion engines may decrease in the West, demand for liquified petroleum gas, naptha, and ethane will likely grow, and the petrochemical industry will see continued expansion, especially in emerging markets (Mehd, 2021).

In new opportunities, some oil and gas producers in the Middle East will lead innovation in technology to enhance hydrocarbon extraction, making it cleaner to produce. "Designer hydrocarbons" will help meet emissions targets and stand out to consumers, along with providing efficiencies for producers and their revenue streams. For example, in Oman, the Miraah project uses solar power to generate steam for advanced oil recovery (Petroleum Development Oman, n.d.). And there are projects in Saudi Arabia advancing carbon capture techniques to convert CO_2 emissions into feedstock for petrochemicals (SABIC, n.d.). But the ability to buy and use new technology is not the same as mastering it for export and dominance across the regional market. Here there is tremendous opportunity for investment and competition to meet the region's economic growth challenges.

The Gulf States to the Rescue? Post-Covid Recovery and Energy Market Upswings

In early 2022, the Gulf economies had some reprieve after the oil demand shock of the Covid-19 pandemic, but there remain some substantial headwinds. While there is some relief at the rebound of oil prices for producers, this comes as a double-edged sword in the region, as we see rising prices across goods and services, commodities, and especially higher food prices.

For oil and gas importers, this creates additional barriers to economic growth and presents a greater burden on cost-of-living expenses to lower-income households. Consumer price index growth is expected to be about 5.8 percent in 2022, which is substantial, but a reprieve from the 11.3 percent growth experienced in 2021, according to estimates by IHS Markit (Naayem, 2021). So, while the average GDP growth expectation is favorable (the IMF estimates regional GDP growth in 2022 at just over 4 percent) there are wide variations across countries in growth expectations (IMF, 2021c). And those expected to achieve very high growth rates, like Iraq for example, are coming from a major contraction, so the rate of economic activity change is less important than the actual expectation of new investment and possible job growth.

The unevenness of economic growth is related to the differences in sources of revenue, especially for oil and gas exporters, but also in government fiscal capacity. Some governments are simply in a more difficult position to access capital, whether in the form of direct financial support or new loans. Many MENA states are now in a position where they are regularly depending on injections of capital, as central bank deposits or commitments of foreign direct investment, from the Gulf states. This is a problem because unlike a finance agreement from the IMF, there is no regular schedule to Gulf support. It is more volatile and commitments of investment are not equal to cash in hand. An oil price boom can strengthen Gulf reserves, but their own financing needs and new infrastructure and clean energy commitments at home will be prioritized.

Turkey's financial distress is one prime example in which Gulf state support would be welcomed, but has not arrived in the form of a central bank deposit, which is most needed to help defend the value of the lira. Instead, we see UAE interest in buying up reduced price assets and a currency swap commitment (Kozok, 2021). Qatar also committed to a currency swap line, but this too is less than is probably desired from Turkey (*Daily Sabah*, 2021).

Jordan is also now reliant on an IMF package (with $400 million in an extended finance facility) and new $1 billion Eurobond debt issuance to help with its external financing needs in 2022 (IMF, 2021b). The Covid-19 pandemic continues to influence the ability of MENA states to garner tourism foreign exchange revenue, and Jordan will be sensitive to any variant disruptions this spring and summer. And while the Jordanian current account deficit will narrow in 2022, the trajectory continues in which there is a constant need for external finance, including direct financial support from the Gulf states.

In Egypt we see another headwind related to global borrowing costs, as its vibrant portfolio investment destination is threatened by a rise in interest rates in the United States, which may create some pressure for capital to exit emerging markets once advanced economies raise their interest rates. Central banks in the region, and especially in Egypt, will be watching closely to manage inflation and exchange rates. Egypt has also recently raised the price of subsidized cooking oil and local fuel in October 2021, which adds to already existing consumer price pressures (Zawya, 2021a). Price control management will continue to constrain fiscal policy and is a pressure point in domestic politics. And like Jordan, tourism inflows will be vulnerable to continued pandemic variants.

The outlook, then, is that inflationary pressures are hurting everyday citizens and consumers, while governments flush with new oil receipts will be focused on spending at home and targeted acquisitions abroad. If interest rates start to go up, the cost of capital will increase for those countries with persistent fiscal deficits. And those MENA economies that have enjoyed strong portfolio inflows may see a risk of capital flight to advanced economies. For MENA economies already in crisis, 2022 could be a difficult year for restructuring debt and accessing new sources of support, especially for Lebanon and Iraq. For Yemen, price pressure will do its worst on the humanitarian situation and food poverty.

Reform and Recovery Models Inside the GCC

Given the trauma of the Covid-19 pandemic, the Gulf states realized a major success in the containment of the virus, a roll-out of a vaccination campaign, and choosing to continue a general shift toward economic reform that began after the decline in oil prices in late 2014. It has been a heavy order for state capacity, and the GCC states have largely demonstrated that their control over population mobility and their tools for management of public health systems have demonstrated competent public service delivery. The reward for that success may be a sharp U-turn in the direction of oil prices by late 2021 that would help with fiscal spending buffers but will also tempt governments to limit their commitment to subsidy reform, taxation, and reduction of the public sector wage bill. However, the economic reform agenda underway in efforts to increase new forms of non-oil government revenue and to reduce government spending on subsidies and public sector wages seems to be holding in place. In general terms, the Covid-19 crisis also highlighted the limits of public sector driven economic growth. The ability to direct support to workers and private sector businesses was comparatively weaker in the Gulf than in OECD and advanced economies.

The future of economic growth in the GCC is looking better just two years later, compared to what some analysts expected in the depths of the downturn in 2020. The Covid-19 pandemic was a twin crisis in the Gulf, as it simultaneously sent a shock to oil prices due to declining demand first from Asia and then globally and hit domestic economic activity through lockdowns and an exit of foreign workers. For oil exporters across the Middle East, the IMF estimates fiscal deficits widened to 10.1 per cent of GDP in 2020 (from 3.8 per cent of GDP in 2019) but are expected to improve significantly in the medium term, reflecting expected higher oil revenue in 2021 (IMF, 2021c). Forecasts now see a rebound in 2021 to strengthen to around 3 percent GDP growth after contracting by 5 percent in 2020 (The World Bank, 2021b). The most surprising recovery has been in non-oil economic growth, which in Saudi Arabia is recovering to 3.9 percent GDP in 2021, according to the Saudi Central Bank (Asharq Al-Awsat, 2021).

What is different in this recovery compared to previous economic crises is a more limited fiscal policy space. In the Global Financial Crisis

(GFC) of 2008–2009, oil prices quickly rebounded, and governments had comfortable reserve assets, as well as fiscal surpluses and very little external debt. In over a decade since the GFC, a lot has changed. Governments in the Gulf continued spending trajectories, took advantage of international debt capital markets, and only recently began the difficult process of reining in energy subsidies and cutting the public sector wage bill. The buffers or reservoirs of support to that existed within national reserves and even the availability of regional support from neighbors is not the same.

Going into the pandemic, oil producers in the Gulf were already under pressure from weak external demand and lower oil prices since the impact of the shale oil revolution in late 2014 (First Abu Dhabi Bank, 2019). Since December 2016, "OPEC plus" cooperation has been in effect, in which Russia and OPEC members led by Saudi Arabia have tried to limit output to buoy oil prices into a more comfortable range around $60 per barrel, but still below many countries' break-even fiscal prices. The impact of the Covid-19 pandemic, along with a battle for market share early in the pandemic in March 2020, nearly derailed that "OPEC plus" cooperation (Stevens, 2020). Moreover, the ability of governments to respond to the Covid-19 crisis has come after five years of more precarious current account balances, with stubborn fiscal deficits that have been financed with rising public debt levels. According to the IMF, the GCC's average public debt-to-GDP ratio rose from 16.2 percent in 2006 to 41.4 percent in 2020 (IMF, 2020). In cases like Oman, debt-to-GDP is closer to 80 percent and even higher in Bahrain (The World Bank, 2021b; Fitch Ratings, 2021). Remarkably, the OPEC plus cooperation agreement has held through 2021 and seen a rebound in oil prices to $85 per barrel, perhaps beyond even the greatest expectations. That volatility though only underscores the problem of a future of oil dependency: it is no way to plan fiscal policy.

The temptation to increase spending resurged as oil prices again rose in late 2021, rebounding to a level approaching or exceeding $70 per barrel in summer of 2021, and then $90 by January 2022. In some cases, like in Oman, in spring 2021 public protests over lack of employment opportunity increased pressure on the government to scale back some austerity measures and create programs to support public employment (Barbuscia & El Yaakoubi, 2021). There is simply more expected of governments in the recovery from Covid-19, but the resources to extend support are more limited, or require difficult choices that jeopardize future spending.

Within the GCC, wage support to private sector workers was limited during the pandemic, given that Gulf citizens are more likely to be public sector workers and foreigners dominate much of the private sector. The Saudi program SANED, an unemployment insurance stipend, was one exception. But, SANED was rolled out at the same time as a general paring back of the existing Citizens Account program, meant to provide monthly assistance to low-income families. Instead, governments tended to direct support toward utility subsidies or reduced fees, edging back at least temporarily on some subsidy reform (Nereim, 2021). This form of pandemic economic relief also tended to be distributed to state-related entities as much as small and medium-sized enterprises, which may have needed the support more. The same distribution of support occurred in the bank sector, as central banks eased lending requirements to the private bank sector and encouraged looser debt repayment terms, to the benefit of large and state-related entities. Across the Gulf, government mandated lockdowns were strict, and while Dubai opened partially to capture tourism revenue over the New Year holiday, most of the GCC remained under travel restrictions through June 2021, including restrictions on religious tourism in Saudi Arabia. One positive effect of lockdowns has been a demonstration of government competence in curtailing the spread of the Covid-19 disease and rolling out vaccination programs effectively.

In some cases, the Covid-19 pandemic accelerated efforts to generate new sources of revenue through taxes and fees. The effect was jarring for some, especially in Saudi Arabia, as the recently introduced value added tax was hiked from 5 percent to 15 percent in July 2020. The introduction of VAT in Oman (April 2021), Bahrain, the UAE, and Saudi Arabia has also contributed to some inflationary pressures. In Saudi Arabia, prices in April 2021 rose 5.3 percent year-on-year from 2020, with food and beverages rising 8.4 percent year-on-year, according to Jadwa Investment research (Jadwa, 2021).

In the future, the possibility of more subdued oil demand and prices suggests that it will be more difficult for GCC countries to rely on oil exports revenues for their continued economic growth. The global energy transition is an opportunity for Gulf national oil companies to become renewable energy giants, and to focus on the downstream products of their natural resource wealth, including petrochemicals and new products like blue and green hydrogen. The challenge for GCC governments will be to accelerate productivity growth among a national labor force. The generation of economic growth over the last three decades has been incredible in many ways: the size of the GCC economies has grown from $0.15 trillion in nominal GDP in 1986 to nearly $1.7 trillion in 2019 (First Abu Dhabi Bank, 2019). Supporting that economic expansion has been growth in infrastructure, education, social services, and public sector employment opportunity. Lower cost imported labor has been a boost to growth, but not necessarily productivity gains over time. That growth curve is now flattening.

Looking Outward, Looking Forward on Climate Policy and Investment Opportunity

How the Gulf states might offer support will likely continue to build on the same toolkit of aid, central bank support, promises of investment, and a bridge to their own industry interests, especially in power and energy products. What these states might hope to achieve with that economic engagement is less certain. Climate adaptation measures and a reckoning with domestic oil and overall energy consumption could also challenge foreign policy practices and the ways that Gulf states choose to engage their region.

The United Arab Emirates has announced it will commit to eliminating carbon emissions within its borders by 2050, the "net-zero" goal in the run up to the COP26 meeting in Glasgow in November 2021 (Reuters, 2021b). Sheikh Mohammed bin Rashid al Maktoum, prime minister of the UAE and ruler of Dubai made the announcement, saying: "We are committed to seize the opportunity to cement our leadership on climate change within our region and take this key economic opportunity to drive development, growth and new jobs." He also committed to a clean energy investment push in the country.

The key phrases to the announcement are "within its borders" and "clean energy." So, while the UAE will continue to be an important global exporter of oil and gas, its own emissions calculations are based on what is used or burned inside of the country. The ability to use the revenues from oil exports to fund a national economic diversification project, including financing for renewable energy domestically and to be able to deploy that technology and capacity abroad as an investor and operator, is a key goal of the new national growth agenda "Project of the 50."

The government is prioritizing its economic growth above foreign policy interventions, and its idea of sustainable growth is a reckoning that while oil and gas are key drivers of the global economy in the short and medium term, the longer-term outlook has less of a role for those products. The net-zero emissions target is on brand for the UAE in its efforts to distinguish itself among its regional peers and to promote the country as a host of international institutions and convenings, including a possible host of a future conference as part of the UN Framework Convention on Climate Change. The UAE, like most of the Gulf states, has some of the world's highest global emissions per capita. The net-zero emissions target will mean some major changes for domestic industry beyond hydrocarbon extraction, like aluminum and manufacturing. For corporates and households, there are bound to be changes in normalization of pricing of energy, from gasoline to electricity. For domestic power production, more reliance on nuclear and solar electricity generation will be a priority.

Saudi Arabia took a similar step in late 2021 to announce a 2060 net-zero emissions target (Krane & Young, 2021). A serious net-zero ambition requires a total overhaul of a fossil fuel driven society and economy in less than four decades. Sweeping changes would affect consumption, almost certainly requiring a revocation of a range of fuel and utility subsidies. The transformation would upend the kingdom's electricity generation, with the construction of new solar power plants along with storage, charging, and a deepened grid to electrify the kingdom. The old business would still have a role, as Saudi oil and gas can be reserved for use as an industrial feedstock or an export commodity.

The result of these massive reconfigurations of Gulf petrostates will be either a diminished reserve for aid and external investment as a tool of foreign policy, or a masterful push to dominate renewables and, at the same time, dominate what remains of the oil market. In either scenario, the Gulf states are leaning into a national development model that accepts risk, demands more of citizens, and extends less in services and benefits from the state. This is likely to be a transferrable set of policy objectives in where and how they offer assistance, and how they prioritize state investments abroad.

For the universe of accessible capital and development finance in the Middle East and Africa, this is a transformative moment. One could consider it a reshaping of the narrative of development from the post-war era in which international financial institutions and a shared sense of how to grow is now upturned.

In Ha-Joon Chang's 2002 book, *Kicking Away the Ladder*, he described a development paradigm geared for the industrialized nations to their benefit which excluded pathways to growth and finance for post-colonial states. Scholars who criticized development discourse of the 1980s and 1990s may be surprised to find that today's challenge is not in the generation of ideas from within developing economies or the Global South for their own national economic strategies (Escobar, 2011). Much of the critique of the Washington Consensus and ideas about institutionalization and the way to support private sector growth is now displaced by a bigger choice set—the whims of the state master developer. The politics are essentially the same: those states with the resources to intervene and shape the political economies within their sphere of influence will do so and to their own interests. The difference is the narrative and intention for global markets. No longer is there a predication that more open economies will create shared growth. This new development model is more nationalistic, perhaps even mercantilist in orientation. And it is set to reshape geopolitics and energy markets for the next few decades.

BIBLIOGRAPHY

Abdelaziz, K., 2019. *Sudan says it has reduced troops in Yemen to 5,000*. [Online] Available at: https://www.reuters.com/article/us-sudan-politics/sudan-says-it-has-reduced-troops-in-yemen-to-5000-idUSKBN1YC0H4

Abdelaziz, K., Georgy, M. & Dahan, M. E., 2019. *Abandoned by the UAE, Sudan's Bashir was destined to fall*. [Online] Available at: https://www.reuters.com/investigates/special-report/sudan-bashir-fall/

Acemoglu, D. & Robinson, J. A., 2012. *Economic Origins of Dictatorship and Democracy*, 8th edition. Cambridge: Cambridge University Press.

Acharya, A., 2004. How Ideas Spread: Whose Norms Matter? Norm Localization and Institutional Change in Asian Regionalism. *International Organization*, 58(2), pp. 239–275.

ADGM, n.d. *Abu Dhabi Global Markets Courts*. [Online] Available at: https://www.adgm.com/adgm-courts [Accessed 21 September 2021].

Afzal, A., Mirze, N. & Arshad, F., 2021. Pakistan's Poverty Puzzle: Role of Foreign Aid, Democracy & Media. *Economic Research-Ekonomska Istraživanja*, 34(1), pp. 368–382.

Aguinaldo, J., 2018. *Chinese contractors are becoming a dominant force*. [Online] Available at: https://www.meed.com/chinese-contractors-relentless-pursuit-bears-fruit/

Aguinaldo, J., 2021. *Chinese firm appointed for Saudi solar schemes*. [Online] Available at: https://www.meed.com/chinese-firm-appointed-for-saudi-solar-schemes

Ahmed, F. Z., 2012. The Perils of Unearned Foreign Income: Aid, Remittances, and Government Survival. *The American Political Science Review*, 106(1), pp. 146–165.

Al Arabiya News, 2015a. *Gulf states offer $12.5 billion aid to Egypt*. [Online] Available at: https://english.alarabiya.net/business/economy/2015/03/13/Saudi-announces-4-billion-aid-package-to-Egypt

Al Arabiya News, 2015b. *UAE official slams "contradictory" Pakistan vote*. [Online] Available at: https://english.alarabiya.net/News/middle-east/2015/04/11/UAE-FM-Pakistan-needs-a-clear-a-position-on-Yemen-conflict-

Al Rajhi Capital, 2020. *Monthly Economic Report: August 2020*. Riyadh: Al-Rajhi Bank.

Aldar, 2020. *Annual Report*. [Online] Available at: https://www.aldar.com/en/investors/reports

American Enterprise Institute, 2021. *Gulf financial aid and direct investment: Tracking the implications of state capitalism, aid, and investment flows.* [Online] Available at: https://www.aei.org/research-products/report/gulf-financial-aid-and-direct-investment-tracking-the-implications-of-state-capitalism-aid-and-investment-flows/

Amwaj Media, 2021. *Surprise meeting in Saudi Arabia highlights shifting Gulf dynamics.* [Online] Available at: https://amwaj.media/media-monitor/red-sea-meeting-highlights-improving-gulf-relations-since-al-ula-summit [Accessed 22 September 2021].

Anon., 2021. *Author Interview* [Interview] (October 2021).

Anwar, H., 2011. *Pakistan Says Adequate Reserves Reduce Need for New IMF Loan.* [Online] Available at: https://www.bloomberg.com/news/articles/2011-09-19/pakistan-says-adequate-reserves-cut-need-for-new-imf-loan-1-?sref=euelgVQS

AP News, 2020. *JinkoSolar Sells Its Stake in Abu Dhabi Sweihan Power Station.* [Online].

Arab News, 2017. *Qatari ships will be barred from using Egyptian ports and the canal's economic zone: official.* [Online] Available at: https://www.arabnews.com/node/1126271/middle-east

Arabian Business, 2018. *China's Silk Road Fund to invest in Dubai solar project.* [Online] Available at: https://www.arabianbusiness.com/industries/energy/401242-chinas-silk-road-fund-to-invest-in-dubai-solar-project

Arnold, T., 2014. *Arabtec's $40bn project in Egypt to open wave of UAE investments.* [Online] Available at: https://www.thenationalnews.com/business/arabtec-s-40bn-project-in-egypt-to-open-wave-of-uae-investments-1.567889

Arvai, Z., Prasad, A. & Katayama, K., 2014. *Macroprudential Policy in the GCC Countries.* London: International Monetary Fund. [Online] Available at: https://www.imf.org/en/Publications/Staff-Discussion-Notes/Issues/2016/12/31/Macroprudential-Policy-in-the-GCC-Countries-40781

Asharq Al-Awsat, 2021. *Saudi Non-Oil GDP Growth Forecast to Grow 3.9% in 2021.* [Online] Available at: https://english.aawsat.com/home/article/2954046/saudi-non-oil-gdp-growth-forecast-grow-39-2021

Ashford, E., 2021. Strategies of Restraint: Remaking America's Broken Foreign Policy. [Online] *Foreign Affairs,* September/October. Available at: https://www.foreignaffairs.com/articles/united-states/2021-08-24/strategies-restraint

Asian Infrastructure Investment Bank, n.d. *Members and Prospective Members of the Bank.* [Online] Available at: https://www.aiib.org/en/about-aiib/governance/members-of-bank/index.html

Asian News International, 2021. *Pakistan's Gwadar loses shine as Saudis shift billion-dollar oil refinery to Karachi.* [Online] Available at: https://www.wionews.com/south-asia/pakistans-gwadar-loses-shine-as-saudis-shift-billion-dollar-oil-refinery-to-karachi-391300

Associated Press in Cairo, 2016. *Egypt devalues currency by 48% to meet IMF demands for $12bn loan.* [Online] Available at: https://www.theguardian.com/world/2016/nov/03/egypt-devalues-currency-meet-imf-demands-loan

Bailey, R. & Willoughby, R., 2013. *Edible Oil: Food Security in the Gulf.* [Online] Available at: https://www.chathamhouse.org/sites/default/files/public/ Research/Energy%2C%20Environment%20and%20Development/ bp1113edibleoil.pdf

Baker McKenzie, 2017. *Belt & Road: Opportunity & Risk.* [Online] Available at: https://www.bakermckenzie.com/-/media/files/insight/publications/2017/10/ belt-road/baker_mckenzie_belt_road_report_2017.pdf

Baldwin, D., 1985. *Economic Statecraft.* Princeton: Princeton University Press.

Baloch, S., 2021. *Hunting rare birds in Pakistan to feed the sex drive of princes.* [Online] Available at: https://www.bbc.com/news/world-asia-56419597

Bank Nizwa, 2021. *Was Oman's banking sector resilient enough to support economic stability during the pandemic?.* Muscat: Oxford Business Group. [Online] Available at: https://oxfordbusinessgroup.com/news/report-was-oman-banking-sector-resilient-enough-support-economic-stability-during-pandemic

Barakat, S. & Zyck, S. A., 2010. *Gulf State Assistance to Conflict-affected Environments.* London: London School of Economics and Political Science.

Barbuscia, D. & Al Sayegh, H., 2020. *ANALYSIS-Arabtec collapse shakes foundations of Gulf construction business.* [Online] Available at: https://www. nasdaq.com/articles/analysis-arabtec-collapse-shakes-foundations-of-gulf-construction-business-2020-10-07

Barbuscia, D. & El Yaakoubi, A., 2021. *Oman orders speedier job creation amid protests over unemployment.* [Online] Available at: https://www.reuters.com/ world/middle-east/job-seeking-omanis-protest-again-press-cash-strapped-government-2021-05-25/

Barclays, 2021. *GCC Contrasting Fiscal Performance.* London: Barclays.

BARWA, 2021. *Home.* [Online] Available at: https://www.barwa.com.qa/en/

Bassam, F. & El-Katiri, L., 2017. A brief political economy of energy subsidies in the Middle East and North Africa. In: G. Luciani, ed. *Combining Economic and Political Development.* Leiden: Brill, pp. 58–87.

BBC, 2011. *Oman uncovers "spy network" but UAE denies any links.* [Online] Available at: https://www.bbc.com/news/world-middle-east-12320859

Bearce, D. H. & Tirone, D. C., 2010. Foreign Aid Effectiveness and the Strategic Goals of Donor Governments. *The Journal of Politics,* 72(3), pp. 837–851.

Bhatia, N., 2020. *Chinese firm wins Etihad Rail wagons deal.* [Online] Available at: https://www.meed.com/chinese-company-wins-etihad-rail-wagons-deal

Bordoff, J. & O'Sullivan, M. L., 2022. *Green Upheaval: The New Geopolitics of Energy.* [Online] *Foreign Affairs,* January/February. Available at: https://www. foreignaffairs.com/articles/world/2021-11-30/geopolitics-energy-green-upheaval

BP plc, 2014. *BP Statistical Review of World Energy,* 63rd edition, London: BP plc [Online] Available at: http://large.stanford.edu/courses/2014/ph240/ milic1/docs/bpreview.pdf

BP plc, 2018. *BP Statistical Review of World Energy,* 67th edition, London: BP plc [Online] Available at: https://www.bp.com/content/dam/bp/business-sites/

en/global/corporate/pdfs/energy-economics/statistical-review/bp-stats-review-2018-full-report.pdf

Bridge, S., 2018. *UAE's ADNOC signs major LNG sales deal with China's Wanhua*. [Online] Available at: https://www.arabianbusiness.com/industries/energy/407837-uaes-adnoc-signs-long-term-lng-sales-deal-with-chinas-wanhua

Brookings Institution, 2019. *Red Sea rivalries: The Gulf, the Horn, and the new geopolitics of the Red Sea*. [Online] Available at: https://www.brookings.edu/events/red-sea-rivalries-the-gulf-the-horn-and-the-new-geopolitics-of-the-red-sea/

Buchanan, J. M. & Tollison, R. D., 1984. *The Theory of Public Choice—II*. Ann Arbor: University of Michigan Press.

Burnside, C. & Dollar, D., 2000. Aid, Policies, and Growth. *American Economic Review*, 90(4), pp. 847–868.

Business Gateways, 2017. *$3.2b invested on China-Oman Industrial Park in Duqm*. [Online] Available at: https://businessgateways.com/news/2017/08/13/Investment-on-China-Oman-Industrial-Park-in-Duqm

Cannon, B. & Rossiter, A., 2018. Ethiopia, Berbera Port and the Shifting Balance of Power in the Horn of Africa. *Rising Powers Quarterly*, 2(4), pp. 7–29.

Carvalho, S., 2018. *Oman's SWF gets approval for $1bln infrastructure fund-official*. [Online] Available at: https://www.zawya.com/mena/en/economy/story/Omans_SWF_gets_approval_for_1bln_infrastructure_fund_official-TR20180118nL8N1PD32OX2/

CEIC, 2020. *Saudi Arabia Foreign Direct Investment*. [Online] Available at: https://www.ceicdata.com/en/indicator/saudi-arabia/foreign-direct-investment

Chadwick, V., 2021. *UAE membership raises human rights concerns around EBRD*. [Online] Available at: https://www.devex.com/news/uae-membership-raises-human-rights-concerns-around-ebrd-98987

Chang, H.-J., 2002. *Kicking Away the Ladder: Development Strategy in Historical Perspective*, 1st edition. London: Anthem Press.

Cheng, E., 2021. *China's aging population is a bigger challenge than its "one-child" policy, economists say*. [Online] Available at: https://www.cnbc.com/2021/03/01/chinas-aging-population-is-bigger-problem-than-one-child-policy-economists.html

Chin, G. T. & Gallagher, K. P., 2019. Coordinated Credit Spaces: The Globalization of Chinese Development Finance. *Development and Change*, 50(1), pp. 245–274.

China Africa Research Initiative, n.d. [Online] Available at: http://www.sais-cari.org/

Clarion Energy, 2019. *ACWA Power building 250 MW solar PV in Ethiopia*. [Online] Available at: https://www.power-eng.com/solar/acwa-power-building-250-mw-in-solar-pv-to-ethiopia/#gref

Cochrane, L., 2021. The United Arab Emirates as a Global Donor: What a Decade of Foreign Aid Data Transparency Reveals. *Development Studies Research*, 8(1), pp. 49–62.

Collier, P., 2006. Is Aid Oil? An Analysis of Whether Africa Can Absorb More Aid. *World Development*, 34(9), pp. 1482–1497.

Cooper, A. F. & Momani, B., 2009. The Challenge of Re-branding Progressive Countries in the Gulf and Middle East: Opportunities through New Networked Engagements versus Constraints of Embedded Negative Images. *Place Branding and Public Diplomacy*, 5, pp. 103–117.

Cornwell, A. & Browning, N., 2018. *UAE denounces siezure of cash and plane in Somalia*. [Online] Available at: https://www.reuters.com/article/us-somalia-politics-emirates/uae-denounces-seizure-of-cash-and-plane-in-somalia-idUSKBN1HH21V [Accessed 15 September 2021].

Costalli, S., Pischedda, C. & Moretti, L., 2017. The Economic Costs of Civil War: Synthetic Counterfactual Evidence and the Effects of Ethnic Fractionalization. *Journal of Peach Research*, 54(1), pp. 80–98.

Daily Sabah, 2021. *Qatar, Turkey extend currency swap deal for another 3 years*. [Online] Available at: https://www.dailysabah.com/business/finance/qatar-turkey-extend-currency-swap-deal-for-another-3-years

Dale, S. & Fattouh, B., 2018. *Peak Oil Demand and Long-Term Oil Prices*, London: BP plc [Online] Available at: https://www.bp.com/content/dam/bp/business-sites/en/global/corporate/pdfs/energy-economics/bp-peak-oil-demand-and-long-run-oil-prices.pdf

Dehn, J., 2019. *The Case for EM External Debt: The Emerging View*. [Online] Available at: www.ashmoregroup.com/sites/default/files/article-docs/EV_May19Thecase- for-EM-external-debt.pdf [Accessed 22 September 2021].

Dhue, S., 2019. *China still borrows billions in low-cost loans from World Bank, as Trump Administration Pushes Back*. [Online] Available at: https://www.cnbc.com/2019/01/09/china-no-longer-a-poor-nation-still-borrows-billions-from-world-bank.html

Drezner, D. W., 2021. The United States of Sanctions: The Use and Abuse of Economic Coercion. *Foreign Affairs*, September/October. [Online] Available at: https://www.foreignaffairs.com/articles/united-states/2021-08-24/united-states-sanctions

Dubai International Finance Centre, 2016. *Growing UAE-China Trade Complements Dubai International Financial Centre Growth Strategy*. [Online] Available at: https://www.difc.ae/newsroom/news/growing-uae-china-trade-complements-dubai-international-financial-centre-growth-strategy/

Dubai Islamic Bank, 2021. *DIB through the Years*. [Online] Available at: https://www.dib.ae/about-us/investor-relations/company-information

Eagle Hills, n.d. *Eagle Hills: About Us*. [Online] Available at: https://www.eaglehills.com/about-us/

Easterly, W. R., 2001. *The Elusive Quest for Growth*. Cambridge: MIT Press.

Easterly, W. R., 2008. *Reinventing Foreign Aid*. Cambridge: MIT Press.

Egypt State Information Service, 2017. *UAE Ambassdor: UAE investments in Egypt ranked first*. [Online] Available at: https://www.sis.gov.eg/Story/113437?lang=en-us

Elhamy, A., 2021. *Oman introduces long-term residencies for foreign investors*. [Online] Available at: https://www.reuters.com/world/middle-east/oman-offers-up-10-year-residency-foreign-investors-trade-ministry-2021-06-23/ [Accessed 22 September 2021].

Energy Egypt, 2017. *Platts: LNG trade disruption worries ease as Qatari flows to Suez, Egypt resume*. [Online] Available at: https://energyegypt.net/platts-lng-trade-disruption-worries-ease-as-qatari-flows-to-suez-egypt-resume/

England, A. & Omran, A., 2020. *Saudi prince powers ahead with futuristic city and sports giga-projects*. [Online] Available at: https://www.ft.com/content/c0c47647-4fc3-4b67-901e-3d4438f42ada

Escobar, A., 2011. *Encountering Development: The Making and Unmaking of the Third World*. Princeton: Princeton University Press.

European Commission, n.d. *Morocco Green Economy Financing Facility (GEFF)*. [Online] Available at: https://ec.europa.eu/eu-external-investment-plan/projects/morocco-green-economy-financing-facility-geff_en

Fattah, Z., 2021. *Top UAE Official Warns on Risk of "Cold War" Between China, U.S.*. [Online] Available at: https://www.bloomberg.com/news/articles/2021-10-02/top-uae-official-warns-on-risk-of-cold-war-between-china-u-s?sref=euelgVQS

Faucon, B. & Nissenbaum, D., 2022. *Houthis Fired Drones and Missiles in Abu Dhabi Attack, Investigation Finds*. [Online] Available at: https://www.wsj.com/articles/houthis-fired-barrage-of-drones-and-missiles-in-abu-dhabi-attack-investigation-finds-11642515339?mod=hp_featst_pos3

Financial Times Ltd., 2021. *fDi Markets*. [Online] Available at: https://report.fdiintelligence.com

First Abu Dhabi Bank, 2019. *GCC Facts and Figures 2019*. [Online] Available at: https://www.bankfab.com/-/media/fabgroup/home/cib/market-insights/macro-strategy-and-economic-update/pdf/fab-gcc-faqs-and-figures-2019.pdf?view=1

Fitch Ratings, 2021. *Fitch revises Oman's outlook to stable*. [Online] Available at: https://www.fitchratings.com/research/sovereigns/fitch-revises-oman-outlook-to-stable-affirms-at-bb-20-12-2021

Forest, E. E., 2018. *Chinese visitor surge set to boost UAE*. [Online] Available at: https://www.thenationalnews.com/business/travel-and-tourism/chinese-visitor-surge-set-to-boost-uae-1.702547

France24, 2020. *Qatar announces new, easier property visa scheme*. [Online] Available at: https://www.news24.com/fin24/economy/world/qatar-announces-new-easier-property-visa-scheme-20201111 [Accessed 22 September 2021].

France 24, 2021. *Iran, Hezbollah aid Yemen rebel strikes: Saudi-led coalition*. [Online] Available at: https://www.france24.com/en/live-news/20211226-iran-hezbollah-aid-yemen-rebel-strikes-saudi-led-coalition

Fulton, J., 2018. *China's power in the Middle East is rising*. [Online] Available at: https://www.washingtonpost.com/news/monkey-cage/wp/2018/08/09/chinas-rise-in-the-middle-east/

Fulton, J., 2019. *China's Changing Role in the Middle East*, Washington, DC: Atlantic Council. [Online] Available at: https://www.atlanticcouncil.org/wp-content/uploads/2019/06/Chinas_Changing_Role_in_the_Middle_East.pdf

Gallagher, K. P. & Myers, M., 2022. *Global China Initiative*. [Online] Available at: https://www.thedialogue.org/map_list/

Gause, G., 2017. Ideologies, Alliances and Underbalancing in the New Middle East Cold War. *Project on Middle East Political Science (POMEPS)*, 16, pp. 17–20.

Georgy, M. & Kahlin, S., 2015. *Gulf Arabs allies pledge $12 billion to Egypt at summit*. [Online] Available at: https://www.reuters.com/article/egypt-economy-investment/gulf-arab-allies-pledge-12-billion-to-egypt-at-summit-idINKBN0M921520150313

Gerring, J., Kingstone, P., Lange, M. & Sinha, A., 2011. Democracy, History, and Economic Performance: A Case-Study Approach. *World Development*, 39(10), pp. 1735–1748.

Global Infrastructure Hub, 2020. *Addis Ababa—Djibouti Railway*. [Online] Available at: https://www.gihub.org/resources/showcase-projects/addis-ababa-djibouti-railway/

Government of China, 2016. *China's Arab Policy Paper*. [Online] Available at: http://www.china.org.cn/world/2016-01/14/content_37573547.htm

Gul, A., 2017. *Saudis Set to Launch Counterterror Coalition Commanded by Ex-Pakistan General Sharif*. [Online] Available at: https://www.voanews.com/a/saudis-set-to-launch-counterterror-coalition-commanded-by-ex-pakistan-general-sharif/4136572.html

Gul, A., 2019. *China Giving Pakistan $3.5 Billion in Loans, Grants*. [Online] Available at: https://www.voanews.com/a/china-giving-billions-to-pakistan-in-loans-grants/4788478.html

Gulf News, 2018. *Adnoc awards $1.6b contract to China's CNPC*. [Online] Available at: https://gulfnews.com/business/energy/adnoc-awards-16b-contract-to-chinas-cnpc-1.2254117

Halligan, N., 2014. *Fast and Furious: Jassim Alseddiqi*. [Online] Available at: https://www.arabianbusiness.com/gcc/fast-furious-jassim-alseddiqi-566964

Harari, Y. N., 2019. *Welcome to the liberal buffet*. [Online] Available at: https://www.ft.com/content/bcd4f5ce-65ae-11e9-b809-6f0d2f5705f6

Harris, J. M. & Blackwill, R., 2016. *War by Other Means: Geoeconomics and Statecraft*. Cambridge: Harvard University Press.

Hill, G., 2017. *Yemen Endures: Civil War, Saudi Adventurism and the Future of Arabia*. London: Hurst Publishers.

Holland, S. & Bose, N., 2021. *Biden defends Afghanistan decision, blames Afghan army's unwillingness to fight*. [Online] Available at: https://www.reuters.com/world/us/biden-says-us-mission-afghanistan-was-never-supposed-be-nation-building-2021-08-16/

Holleis, J., 2021. *UAE's tourism sector gets a shot in the arm as Israelis flock to Dubai*. [Online] Available at: https://www.dw.com/en/uaes-tourism-sector-gets-a-shot-in-the-arm-as-israelis-flock-to-dubai/a-56217968

Horn, S., Reinhart, C. M. & Trebesch, C., 2019. *China's Overseas Lending*. Working Paper #26050. Cambridge: National Burau of Economic Research. [Online] Available at: https://www.nber.org/papers/w26050

HSBC, 2021. *Oman, A Work in Progress*. [Online].

Hudson, C., 2021. *Time is running out for Abiy's "new beginning" in Ethiopia.* [Online] Available at: https://www.atlanticcouncil.org/blogs/new-atlanticist/time-is-running-out-for-abiys-new-beginning-in-ethiopia/

Humphrey, C. and Chen, Y., 2021. *China in the multilateral development banks: evolving strategies of a new power*, London: ODI. [Online] Available at: https://odi.org/en/publications/china-multilateral-development-banks/

International Holding Company, n.d. *About.* [Online] Available at: https://ihcuae.com/about/index.html#Message

International Monetary Fund (IMF), 2008. *Regional Economic Outlook: Middle East and Central Asia.* [Online] Available at: https://www.imf.org/en/Publications/REO/MECA/Issues/2017/01/07/Regional-Economic-Outlook-Middle-East-and-Central-Asia10

International Monetary Fund (IMF), 2018. *Gulf Cooperation Council: How Developed and Inclusive are Financial Systems in the GCC?.* [Online] Available at: https://www.imf.org/en/Publications/Policy-Papers/Issues/2018/12/04/pp120618gcc-how-developed-and-inclusive-are-financial-systems-in-the-gcc

International Monetary Fund, Middle East and Central Asia Dept. (IMF), 2020. *Economic Prospects and Policy Challenges for the GCC Countries.* [Online] Available at: https://www.imf.org/en/Publications/Policy-Papers/Issues/2020/12/08/Economic-Prospects-and-Policy-Challenges-for-the-GCC-Countries-49942

International Monetary Fund (IMF), 2021a. *Fiscal Monitor April 2021.* [Online] Available at: https://www.imf.org/en/Publications/FM/Issues/2021/03/29/fiscal-monitor-april-2021

International Monetary Fund (IMF), 2021b. *IMF Executive Board Concludes Third Review Under Jordan's Extended Arrangement.* [Online] Available at: https://www.imf.org/en/News/Articles/2021/12/20/pr21391-jordan-imf-executive-board-concludes-third-review-under-extended-arrangement

International Monetary Fund (IMF), 2021c. *Regional Economic Outlook: Middle East and Central Asia.* [Online] Available at: https://data.imf.org/?sk=4cc54c86-f659-4b16-abf5-fab77d52d2e6

Islamic Development Bank, 2018. *FDI in fragile and conflict affected economies in the Middle East and North Africa: trends and policies.* Jeddah: Islamic Development Bank.

Islamic Development Bank, 2021a. *Investing in Green and Resilient Infrastructure Could Create Millions of Green Jobs, Says IsDB Group Chairman at F20 Climate Solutions Forum.* [Online] Available at: https://www.isdb.org/news/investing-in-green-and-resilient-infrastructure-could-create-millions-of-green-jobs-says-isdb-group-chairman-at-f20-climate-solutions-forum

Islamic Development Bank, 2021b. *SDRPY and IsDB Launch Executive Program for Development Cooperation in Yemen.* [Online] Available at: https://www.isdb.org/news/sdrpy-and-isdb-launch-executive-program-for-development-cooperation-in-yemen

Jabarkhyl, N., 2017. *Oman counts on Chinese billions to build desert boomtown.* [Online] Available at: https://www.reuters.com/article/us-oman-china-investment/oman-counts-on-chinese-billions-to-build-desert-boomtown-idUSKCN1BG1WJ

Jadwa, 2021. *Monthly Chartbook.* [Online] Available at: http://www.jadwa.com/en/researchsection/research/chart-books

Jones, S. G., Thompson, J., Ngo, D., McSorley, B. & Bermudez, J. S., Jr., 2021. *The Iranian and Houthi War against Saudi Arabia,* Washington, DC: Center for Strategic and International Studies. [Online] Available at: https://www.csis.org/analysis/iranian-and-houthi-war-against-saudi-arabia

Kawas, M., 2018. *Emirati author chronicles rise of Gulf countries.* [Online] Available at: https://thearabweekly.com/emirati-author-chronicles-rise-gulf-countries

Khan, A. & Kim, Y.-H., 1999. *Foreign Direct Investment in Pakistan: Policy Issues and Operational Implications.* Manila: Asian Development Bank.

Kharas, H. & Desai, R. M., 2020. *The Determinants of Aid Volatility.* Washington, DC: The Brookings Institution.

Kiganda, A., 2020. *Terra Sola to construct 200MW PV module plant in Egypt.* [Online] Available at: https://constructionreviewonline.com/company-reviews/terra-sola-to-construct-200mw-pv-module-plant-in-egypt/

Koch, C., 2017. *Success and Shortcomings of GCC Economic "Vision" Documents* [Online] Available at: https://www.arabdevelopmentportal.com/blog/success-and-shortcomings-gcc-economic-%E2%80%9Cvision%E2%80%9D-documents [Accessed 21 September 2021].

Kozok, F., 2021. *UAE Sets Up $10 Billion Fund to Support Turkey as Ties Warm.* [Online] Available at: https://www.bloomberg.com/news/articles/2021-11-24/uae-turkey-to-sign-financial-cooperation-deals-as-ties-mend?sref=euelgVQS

Kragelund, P., 2008. The Return of Non-DAC Donors to Africa: New Prospects for African Development?. *Development Policy Review,* 26(5), pp. 555–584.

Krane, J. & Young, K. E., 2021. *A net-zero Saudi Arabia? Not so fast.* [Online] Available at: https://www.al-monitor.com/originals/2021/10/net-zero-saudi-arabia-not-so-fast

Kreuger, A. O., 1974. The Political Economy of Rent-Seeking Society. *The American Economic Review,* 64(3), pp. 291–303.

Krishnan, J., 2018. *The Story of the Dubai International Financial Centre Courts.* Dubai: Motivate Publishing.

Kulovic, N., 2021. *ADNOC partners with Pakistani companies for the first time.* [Online] Available at: https://www.offshore-energy.biz/adnoc-partners-with-pakistani-companies-for-the-first-time/

Laessing, U. & Johnston, 2011. *Gulf states launch $20 billion fund for Oman and Bahrain.* [Online] Available at: https://www.reuters.com/article/us-gulf-fund/gulf-states-launch-20-billion-fund-for-oman-and-bahrain-idUSTRE7294B120110310

Li, H., Loyalka, P., Rozelle, S. & Wu, B., 2017. Human Capital and China's Future Growth. *Journal of Econmoic Perspectives,* 31(1), pp. 25–48.

Lipset, S., 1959. Some Social Requisites of Democracy: Economic Development and Political Legitimacy. *American Political Science Review,* 53(1), pp. 69–105.

Litan, D. & Steil, B., 2006. *Financial Statecraft: The Role of Financial Markets in American Foreign Policy*. New Haven: Yale University Press.

Maasho, A., 2018. *UPDATE 1-Ethiopia PM says China will restructure railway loan*. [Online] Available at: https://www.reuters.com/article/ethiopia-china-loan-idUSL5N1VS4IW

Maasho, A. & Kalin, S., 2019. *Saudi Arabia frees Ethiopian-born tycoon amid flurry of releases*. [Online] Available at: https://www.reuters.com/article/us-saudi-arrests/saudi-arabia-frees-ethiopian-born-tycoon-amid-flurry-of-releases-idUSKCN1PL0IA

Marks, S., 2021. *Sudan Taps Gulf Allies as Donor Cuts Worsen Economic Outlook*. [Online] Available at: https://www.bloomberg.com/news/articles/2021-12-17/sudan-taps-gulf-allies-as-donor-cuts-worsen-economic-outlook?sref=euelgVQS

Marlow, I., Martin, P. & Haider, K., 2018. *China's $2 Billion Pakistan Loan Shows Desire to Keep Khan Close*. [Online] Available at: https://www.bloomberg.com/news/articles/2018-08-01/china-s-2-billion-pakistan-loan-shows-desire-to-keep-khan-close?sref=euelgVQS

Martin, M. & Narayanan, A., 2018. *Oman Weighs $2 Billion Loan After Multi-Billion-Dollar Bond*. [Online] Available at: https://www.bloomberg.com/news/articles/2018-01-23/oman-is-said-to-weigh-2-billion-loan-after-multi-billion-bond

Masdar, 2019. *Dhofar Wind Project*. [Online] Available at: https://masdar.ae/en/masdar-clean-energy/projects/dhofar-wind-project

McCartney, M., 2021. *The Dragon from the Mountains: The China-Pakistan Economic Corridor (Cpec) from Kashgar to Gwadar*. Cambridge: Cambridge University Press.

MEED, 2018. *Report: The future of Middle East energy*. [Online] Available at: https://www.meed.com/future-middle-east-energy/

MEED, 2021. *Saudi Arabia to award nuclear advisory deal*. [Online] Available at: https://www.power-technology.com/comment/saudi-arabia-nuclear-advisory-deal/

Mehd, A., 2021. *The Middle East and the geopolitics of the energy transition*. [Online] Available at: https://www.oxfordenergy.org/wpcms/wp-content/uploads/2021/02/THE-MIDDLE-EAST-AND-THE-GEOPOLITICS-OF-THE-ENERGY-TRANSITION-MYTHS-AND-REALITIES-.pdf

Meighan, B., 2016. *Egypt's Natural Gas Crisis*. [Online] Available at: https://carnegieendowment.org/sada/62534

MENA Economic Monitor, 2017. *The Economics of Post-Conflict Reconstruction in MENA*. Washington, DC: The World Bank.

Menon, A., 2014. *China to become GCC's biggest export market*. [Online] Available at: https://meconstructionnews.com/7458/china-to-become-gccs-biggest-export-market

Mills, R., Ishfaq, S., Ibrahim, R. & Reese, A., 2017. *China's Road to the Gulf: Opportunities for the GCC in the Belt and Road initiative*. [Online] Available at: https://emerge85.io/wp-content/uploads/2017/10/Chinas-Road-to-the-Gulf.pdf

Ministry of Information Eritrea, 2018. *Joint Statement on the Eritrean-Ethiopian-UAE Tripartite Summit in Abu Dhabi*. [Online] Available at: https://shabait.com/2018/07/24/joint-statement-on-the-eritrean-ethiopian-uae-tripartite-summit-in-abu-dhabi/

Mohseni-Cheraghlou, A., 2021. *Fossil fuel subsidies and renewable energies in MENA: An oxymoron?* [Online] Available at: https://www.mei.edu/publications/fossil-fuel-subsidies-and-renewable-energies-mena-oxymoron

Molavi, A., 2020. *Enter the Dragon: China's Growing Influence in the Middle East and North Africa*. [Online] Available at: https://www.hoover.org/sites/default/files/research/docs/molavi_webready_revised.pdf

Momani, B. & Ennis, C. A., 2013. Shaping the Middle East in the Midst of the Arab Uprisings: Turkish and Saudi Foreign Policy Strategies. *Third World Quarterly*, 34(6), pp. 1127–1144.

Mooney, T., 2018. *DP World deploys legal attack on Djibouti terminal nationalization*. [Online] Available at: https://www.joc.com/port-news/terminal-operators/dp-world/dp-world-deploys-legal-attack-djibouti-terminal-nationalization_20180912.html

Moore, B., 1966. *Social Origins of Dictatorship and Democracy*. Boston: Princeton University Press.

Mubadala Investment Company, n.d. *PAK-ARAB Refinery (PARCO)*. [Online] Available at: https://www.mubadala.com/en/what-we-do/petroleum-and-petrochemicals/pak-arab-refinery-parco

Mukrashi, F. A., 2017. *75,000 Omanis apply for fuel subsidy scheme*. [Online] Available at: https://gulfnews.com/world/gulf/oman/75000-omanis-apply-for-fuel-subsidy-scheme-1.2145467

Muscat Daily, 2018. *H E Sunaidy woos Indian firms to store food grains in Oman*. [Online] Available at: https://www.pressreader.com/oman/muscat-daily/20180125/281655370499608

Naayem, J., 2021. *MENA economic outlook 2022: Strengthening regional growth faces noticeable global headwinds*. [Online] Available at: https://ihsmarkit.com/research-analysis/mena-economic-outlook-2022-global-headwinds.html#:~:text=IHS%20Markit%20currently%20projects%20average,1.5%25%20during%20the%20same%20period

Nafie, M. & Holtmeier, L., 2020. *GCC to witness exit of expatriate workers due to coronavirus: Experts*. [Online] Available at: https://english.alarabiya.net/coronavirus/2020/04/14/GCC-to-witness-exit-of-expatriate-workers-due-to-coronavirus-Experts-

Nair, D. & Martin, M., 2020. *Saudi Wealth Fund Increases ACWA Stake to 50% Ahead of IPO*. [Online] Available at: https://www.bloombergquint.com/markets/saudi-wealth-fund-said-near-deal-to-boost-acwa-stake-before-ipo

Nair, D. & Narayanan, A., 2017. *Oman to Follow Abu Dhabi With Sovereign Fund Merger Plans*. [Online] Available at: https://www.bloomberg.com/news/articles/2017-04-24/oman-said-to-follow-abu-dhabi-with-sovereign-fund-merger-plans?sref=euelgVQS

Nereim, V., 2021. *Two Million Saudis Lose Cash Aid When They Can Least Afford It*. [Online] Available at: https://www.bloomberg.com/news/articles/

2020-07-15/two-million-saudis-lose-cash-aid-when-they-can-least-afford-it?sref=euelgVQS

Neumayer, E., 2003. What Factors Determine the Allocation of Aid by Arab Countries and Multilateral Agencies?. *The Journal of Development Studies*, 39, pp. 134–147.

New Development Bank, n.d. *NDB'S Member Countries*. [Online] Available at: https://www.ndb.int/about-us/organisation/members/

Newlines Institute, 2020. *China's Syria Policy Could Increase Beijing's Middle East Footprint*. [Online] Available at: https://newlinesinstitute.org/china/chinas-syria-policy-could-increase-beijings-middle-east-footprint/

News Wires, 2021. *Thousands again take to the streets in Sudan to call for return to civilian rule*. [Online] Available at: https://www.france24.com/en/africa/20211225-thousands-of-protesters-in-sudan-call-for-transition-to-civilian-rule

Nonneman, G., 1988. *Development, Administration and Aid in the Middle East*. New York: Routledge.

North, D. C., 1990. *Institutions, Institutional Change and Economic Performance*. Cambridge: Cambridge University Press.

Office of the United Nations High Commissioner for Human Rights, n.d. *Development finance institutions*. [Online] Available at: https://www.ohchr.org/EN/Issues/Development/Pages/DFI.aspx

Offshore Energy, 2018. *Oman Gets Funding from Saudi Arabia to Develop Duqm Port*. [Online] Available at: https://www.offshore-energy.biz/oman-gets-funding-from-saudi-arabia-to-develop-duqm-port/

Oman Sovereign Sukuk S.A.O.C., 2021. *Prospectus*. Oman: S.A.O.C.

Omanuna, n.d. *The National Program for Enhancing Economic Diversification (Tanfeedh): Overview and Goals*. [Online] Available at: https://omanportal.gov.om/wps/portal/index/interact/tanfeedh/!ut/p/a1/hc9Nb4JAEAbgX8OVmV0IQW9TPwENpWsV92LQrCsJsAa38velxksTrXN7J8-bzICEHGRTXEtd2NI0RfWbZbBLMxaweYpJuM4mSF8kMmKcI_o92PYAXwzhu_4G5J2IOPkQkc8xnQqGEUXz0YhWnH0HD-DhDDEdRMtktSTk3noaDxaBNx77D_DPDTFIX
Organization for Economic Cooperation and Development (OPEC), 2018. *FDI in fragile and conflict-affected economies in the Middle East and North Africa: trends and policies*. [Online] Available at: https://www.oecd.org/mena/competitiveness/ERTF-Jeddah-2018-Background-note-FDI.pdf [Accessed 15 September 2021].

Organization for Economic Cooperation and Development (OPEC), n.d. *How Arab Conutries and Institutions Finance Development*. [Online] Available at: https://www.oecd.org/dac/dac-global-relations/Development_finance_Arab_countries_institutions.pdf

Oxford Business Group, n.d. *Dubai Silk Road strategy to capitalise on logistics infrastructure and global connections*. [Online] Available at: https://oxfordbusinessgroup.com/analysis/sleek-strategy-dubai-silk-road-strategy-outlined-mid-2019-aims-capitalise-emirate%E2%80%99s-trade-and

Paola, A. D., 2018. *Saudi Looks to Petrochemicals for Its Next Big Projects.* [Online] Available at: https://www.bloomberg.com/news/articles/2018-10-10/saudis-look-past-crude-with-100-billion-in-downstream-projects?sref=euelgVQS

Parasie, N., 2015. *Egypt Unveils Plans for New Capital City.* [Online] Available at: https://www.wsj.com/articles/egypt-unveils-plans-for-new-capital-city-1426342865

Paravicini, G., Houreld, K. & Endeshaw, D., 2021. *Ethiopia's crackdown on ethnic Tigrayans snares thousands.* [Online] Available at: https://www.reuters.com/investigates/special-report/ethiopia-conflict-tigrayans/

Parker, S. & Chefitz, G., 2018. *Debtbook Diplomacy: China's Strategic Leveraging of its Newfound Economic Influence and the Consequences for U.S. Foreign Policy.* Cambridge: The Harvard Kennedy School.

Patrick, N., 2017. *The Saudi and Emirati Conundrum After Saleh.* [Online] Available at: https://carnegieendowment.org/sada/75054

Paul, K., 2017. *Saudi king approves $19 billion of economic stimulus steps.* [Online] Available at: https://www.reuters.com/article/us-saudi-stimulus/saudi-king-approves-19-billion-of-economic-stimulus-steps-idUSKBN1E80SO?il=0

Petroleum Development Oman, n.d. *Miraah Solar Project.* [Online] Available at: https://www.pdo.co.om/en/technical-expertise/solar-project-miraah/Pages/default.aspx

Pottinger, M., 2021. Beijing's American Hustle. *Foreign Affairs*, September/October. [Online] Available at: https://www.foreignaffairs.com/articles/asia/2021-08-23/beijings-american-hustle

PwC, 2020. *Oman: Oman VAT Law published in the Official Gazette.* [Online] Available at: https://www.pwc.com/m1/en/services/tax/me-tax-legal-news/2020/oman-vat-law-published-in-official-gazette.html

PwC, 2021. *GCC: Immigration roundup from the last 12 months.* [Online] Available at: https://www.pwc.com/m1/en/services/tax/me-tax-legal-news/2021/gcc-immigration-employment-roundup-july-2021.html [Accessed 22 September 2021].

Qian, X. & Fulton, J., 2018. China-Gulf Economic Relationship under the "Belt and Road" Initiative. *Asian Journal of Middle Eastern and Islamic Studies*, 11(3), pp. 12–21.

Rahman, F., 2018. *Cosco built container terminal opens in Abu Dhabi.* [Online] Available at: https://gulfnews.com/business/energy/cosco-built-container-terminal-opens-in-abu-dhabi-1.60856478

Rahman, F., 2021. *Aldar and ADQ consortium to buy 90% of Egyptian developer Sodic.* [Online] Available at: https://www.thenationalnews.com/business/property/2021/09/14/aldar-and-adq-consortium-offers-to-buy-90-of-egyptian-developer-sodic/

Rakhmat, M. Z., 2019. *The Belt and Road Initiative in the Gulf: Building "Oil Roads" to Prosperity.* [Online] Available at: https://www.mei.edu/publications/belt-and-road-initiative-gulf-building-oil-roads-prosperity

Rashed, M., Azhar, S. & Kalin, S., 2020. *Saudi Arabia asked state agencies to prepare for sharp budget cuts—sources*. [Online] Available at: https://www.reuters.com/article/saudi-economy-budget/saudi-arabia-asked-state-agencies-to-prepare-for-sharp-budget-cuts-sources-idINL8N2B35UN

Ratcliffe, V., 2018. *Oman's OQ and Partners Plan 25-Gigawatt Green Hydrogen Plant*. [Online] Available at: https://www.bloomberg.com/news/articles/2021-05-18/oman-s-oq-and-partners-plan-25-gigawatt-green-hydrogen-plant

Ray, R., Gallagher, K. P., Kring, W., Pitts, J. & Simmons, B. A. 2021. Geolocated Dataset of Chinese Overseas Development Finance. *Scientific Data*, 8(241). [Online] Available at: https://doi.org/10.1038/s41597-021-01021-7

Razgallah, B., 2021. *The Political Economy of GCC Financial Support*. London: Barclays.

Reel, M., 2018. *The Irresistible Urge to Build Cities From Scratch*. [Online] Available at: https://www.bloomberg.com/news/features/2018-11-02/the-irresistible-urge-to-build-cities-from-scratch?sref=euelgVQS

Reuters, 2002. *CPECC signs $317m deal with Pakistan*. [Online] Available at: https://gulfnews.com/business/energy/cpecc-signs-317m-deal-with-pakistan-1.382379

Reuters, 2009. *UPDATE 1-Barwa to start $9 bln Cairo project in Q1 2010*. [Online] Available at: https://www.reuters.com/article/barwa-egypt/update-1-barwa-to-start-9-bln-cairo-project-in-q1-2010-idUKLB68078420090811

Reuters, 2012. *Qatar's Barwa to sell $4.4 billion in assets to repay loans*. [Online] Available at: https://www.reuters.com/article/us-barwa-sales/qatars-barwa-to-sell-4-4-billion-in-assets-to-repay-loans-idUSBRE89604I20121007

Reuters, 2016. *Egypt Cenbank pays back $1billion owed to Qatar*. [Online] Available at: https://www.reuters.com/article/egypt-qatar-cenbank/egyptian-cenbank-pays-back-1-billion-debt-owed-to-qatar-idUSL8N19N442

Reuters, 2017a. *Egypt's inflation rises again, and is expected to keep going up*. [Online] Available at: https://www.reuters.com/article/us-egypt-economy-inflation-idUSKBN19V1I7

Reuters, 2017b. *Qatari forces in Saudi-led coalition return home*. [Online] Available at: https://www.reuters.com/article/us-gulf-qatar-alliance/qatari-forces-in-saudi-led-coalition-return-home-idUSKBN18Y2YH

Reuters, 2017c. *UPDATE 1-Oman signs $3.55 billion loan with Chinese banks*. [Online] Available at: https://www.reuters.com/article/oman-loan/update-1-oman-signs-3-55-billion-loan-with-chinese-banks-idUSL5N1KP2XX

Reuters, 2018. *From war room to boardroom. Military firms flourish in Sisi's Egypt*. [Online] Available at: https://www.reuters.com/investigates/special-report/egypt-economy-military/

Reuters, 2020. *Israel sees trade with UAE at $4 billion per year*. [Online] Available at: https://www.reuters.com/article/us-emirates-israel-economy-idUKKBN25Y14B

Reuters, 2021a. *Houthis have fired 430 missiles, 851 drones at Saudi Arabia since 2015—Saudi-led coalition*. [Online] Available at: https://www.reuters.com/

world/middle-east/houthis-have-fired-430-missiles-851-drones-saudi-
arabia-since-2015-saudi-led-2021-12-26/

Reuters, 2021b. *UAE launches plan to achieve net zero emissions by 2050.*
[Online] Available at: https://www.reuters.com/world/middle-east/uae-
launches-plan-achieve-net-zero-emissions-by-2050-2021-10-07/

Reuters, 2021c. [Online] Available at: https://www.reuters.com/article/arabs-
investments-ye6-idARAKCN2E010O

Rouchdy, M. S. & Hamdy, I. A., eds., 2017. The Food Question in the Middle
East. *Cairo Papers in Social Sciences*, 34(4), pp. 127–140.

Saadi, D., 2020. *UAE's ADNOC adds CNOOC of China as new partner in two
offshore concessions.* [Online] Available at: https://www.spglobal.com/platts/
en/market-insights/latest-news/natural-gas/072720-uaes-adnoc-adds-cnooc-
of-china-as-new-partner-in-two-offshore-concessions

Saadi, D., 2021. *ADNOC awards offshore exploration rights to Pakistani
consortium for first time.* [Online] Available at: https://www.spglobal.com/
platts/en/market-insights/latest-news/oil/083121-adnoc-awards-offshore-
exploration-rights-to-pakistani-consortium-for-first-time

SABIC, n.d. *Creating the world's largest carbon capture and utilization plant.*
[Online] Available at: https://www.sabic.com/en/newsandmedia/stories/
our-world/creating-the-worlds-largest-carbon-capture-and-utilization-plant

Sabri, N. R., 2008. *Financial Markets and Institutions in the Arab Economy.* New
York: Nova Science Publishers.

Sahloul, A., 2020. *China's Syria Policy Could Increase Beijing's Middle East
Footprint.* [Online] Available at: https://newlinesinstitute.org/china/
chinas-syria-policy-could-increase-beijings-middle-east-footprint/

Saidi, N., 2018. *Why the GCC should adopt the petroyuan.* [Online] Available at:
https://www.thenationalnews.com/business/comment/why-the-gcc-should-
adopt-the-petroyuan-1.694111

Saldinger, A., 2020. *As OPIC shuts its doors, former leaders reflect.* [Online]
Available at: https://www.devex.com/news/as-opic-shuts-its-doors-former-
leaders-reflect-96346

Salman, N. & Aamir, M., 2018. *Emirates News Agency.* [Online] Available at:
http://wam.ae/en/details/1395302680900 [Accessed 15 September 2021].

Saudi Press Agency, 2018. *Custodian of the Two Holy Mosques Receives Number
of Arab, African Foreign Ministers.* [Online] Available at: https://www.spa.gov.
sa/viewfullstory.php?lang=en&newsid=1852492#1852492

Security Council, 2015. *Resolution 2216.* [Online] Available at: https://www.un.
org/securitycouncil/s/res/2216-%282015%29-0

Seleshie, L., 2021. *Can Ethiopia restructure its debt in the midst of civil war?.*
[Online] Available at: https://www.theafricareport.com/113429/can-
ethiopia-restructure-its-debt-in-the-midst-of-civil-war/

Shaibany, S. A., 2018. *Oman protest: Hundreds demand jobs.* [Online] Available
at: https://www.thenationalnews.com/world/gcc/oman-protest-hundreds-
demand-jobs-1.697750

Shalev, C., 2012. *Dennis Ross: Saudi King vowed to obtain nuclear bomb after
Iran.* [Online] Available at: https://www.haaretz.com/2012-05-30/ty-article/

dennis-ross-saudi-king-vowed-to-obtain-nuclear-bomb-after-iran/0000017f-
f76e-d044-adff-f7ff30de0000

Sheline, A., 2020. *Oman's smooth transition doesn't mean its neighbors won't stir
up trouble.* [Online] Available at: https://foreignpolicy.com/2020/01/23/
omans-smooth-transition-saudi-arabia-uae-mbs-stir-up-trouble/

Shenker, J., 2015. *Sharm el-Sheikh rumbles with grand promises of the
international elite.* [Online] Available at: https://www.theguardian.com/
world/2015/mar/15/egyot-sharma-el-sheikh-rumbles-grand-promises

Shushan, D., 2011. The Rise (and Decline?) of Arab Aid: Generosity and
Allocation in the Oil Era. *World Development,* 39(11), pp. 1969–1980.

Siddiqi, R. A., 2019. Pakistan's Evolving Relations with Saudi Arabia: Emerging
Dynamics and Challenges. *Policy Perspectives,* 16(1), pp. 61–76.

Simmons, A., 1981. *Arab Foreign Aid.* London Associated University Press.

SOHAR, n.d. *Overview.* [Online] Available at: http://www.soharportand
freezone.com/en/about/overview

Sovereign Wealth Fund Institute, 2021. *Oman Investment Authority Goes the
SDSWF Route.* [Online] Available at: https://www.swfinstitute.org/
news/84229/oman-investment-authority-goes-the-sdswf-route

Spencer, B., 2020. *Axilion brings digital twin tech to UAE.* [Online] Available at:
https://www.itsinternational.com/its4/news/axilion-brings-digital-twin-tech-
uae

Stacey, K., Bokhari, F. & Sender, H., 2017. China bails out Pakistan with $1.25bn
loans. *Financial Times,* April 25. [Online] Available at: https://www.ft.com/
content/3ae64c9a-ffd8-11e6-96f8-3700c5664d30

State Council of the People's Republic of China, 2021. *China's International
Development Cooperation in the New Era.* [Online]. Available at: http://
english.www.gov.cn/archive/whitepaper/202101/10/content_
WS5ffa6bbbc6d0f72576943922.html

Stevens, P., 2020. *OPEC and allies agree to historic 10 million barrel per day
production cut.* [Online] Available at: https://www.cnbc.com/2020/04/09/
oil-jumps-ahead-of-make-or-break-opec-meeting.html

Stevenson, P., 2021. *Egypt Calls Time On LNG Exports: End of the Country's Gas
Surplus?.* [Online] Available at: https://www.mees.com/2021/9/17/oil-gas/
egypt-calls-time-on-lng-exports-end-of-the-countrys-gas-surplus/a5fd8d70-
17b5-11ec-af84-fd006eb0a8cd

Stiglitz, J. E. & Greenwald, B. C., 2014. *Creating a Learning Society: A New
Approach to Growth, Development, and Social Progress.* New York: Columbia
Universty Press.

Stiglitz, J. E. & Hoff, K., 2001. Modern Economic Theory and Development.
In: G. Meier & J. E. Stiglitz, eds. *Frontiers of Development Economics: The
Future in Perspective.* Washington: World Bank and Oxford University Press,
pp. 389–459.

Sundar, S., 2019. *Oman bus plant construction contract to be signed in November.*
[Online] Available at: https://www.zawya.com/mena/en/projects/story/
Oman_bus_plant_construction_contract_to_be_signed_in_November-
ZAWYA20191113091707/

Tadesse, F. & Gebre, S., 2021. *U.S. Blocks Duty-Free Trade Access to Ethiopia Over Conflict.* [Online] Available at: https://www.bloomberg.com/news/articles/2021-11-02/u-s-suspends-duty-free-trade-access-to-ethiopia-over-conflict

Tannenbaum, C. R., Boyle, R. J. & Tandon, V., 2020. *Government Debt, Liability, and the She-Cession.* [Online] Available at: https://www.northerntrust.com/united-states/insights-research/2020/market-economic-commentary/wec/august-7

Tan, W., 2019. *About half of China's loans to developing countries are "hidden," study finds.* [Online] Available at: https://www.cnbc.com/2019/07/12/chinas-lending-to-other-countries-jumps-causing-hidden-debt.html

Teng, C. H., Zhu, N. & Herrero, A. G., 2018. *Tighter rules targeting shadow banking put brakes on China banks' expansion.* [Online] Available at: https://asianbankingandfinance.net/retail-banking/exclusive/tighter-rules-targeting-shadow-banking-put-brakes-china-banks-expansion

The Economist, 2019. *UAE's KFED signs strategic partnership with Ethiopia.* [Online] Available at: http://country.eiu.com/article.aspx?articleid=1268251510&Country=Ethiopia&topic=Politics&subtopic_1

The Financial Times, 2017. *State stakes in Gulf banks bring business advantages—and risks.* [Online] Available at: https://www.ft.com/content/ac0789fc-87e1-11e7-8bb1-5ba57d47eff7

The Middle East North Africa Financial Network, 2017. *Oman's $2bn international sukuk oversubscribed more than three times.* [Online] Available at: https://menafn.com/1095537660/Omans-2bn-international-sukuk-oversubscribed-more-than-three-times

The Nobel Prize, 2019. *Abiy Ahmed Ali: Facts.* [Online] Available at: https://www.nobelprize.org/prizes/peace/2019/abiy/facts/

The World Bank, 1993. *The East Asian Miracle: Economic Growth and Public Policy.* Washington, DC: The World Bank.

The World Bank, 1998. *Assessing Aid: What Works, What Doesn't and Why.* Washington, DC: The World Bank.

The World Bank, 2003. *Breaking the Conflict Trap: Civil War and Development Policy.* Washington, DC: The World Bank.

The World Bank, 2018. *Poverty and Shared Prosperity 2018: Piecing Together the Poverty Puzzle.* Washington, DC: The World Bank.

The World Bank, 2019. *Ethiopia Financial Sector Development: The Path to an Efficient Stable and Inclusive Financial Sector.* Washington, DC: The World Bank.

The World Bank, 2020. COVID-19: Remittance Flows to Shrink 14% by 2021, *Press Release.* Washington, DC: The World Bank. [Online] Available at: https://www.worldbank.org/en/news/press-release/2020/10/29/covid-19-remittance-flows-to-shrink-14-by-2021

The World Bank, 2021a. *Pakistan Development Update, April 2021: Navigating in Uncertain Times.* Washington, DC: The World Bank.

The World Bank, 2021b. *GCC Economic Update—April 2021.* [Online] Available at: https://www.worldbank.org/en/country/gcc/publication/economic-update-april-2021

Times of Oman, 2021. *More than 500,000 fixed telephone line subscribers in Oman*. [Online] Available at: https://timesofoman.com/article/97959

Tirone, D. C. & Savun, B., 2012. Exogenous Shocks, Foreign Aid, and Civil War. *International Organization*, 66(3), pp. 363–393.

Tok, E., Calleja, R. & El-Ghaish, H., 2014. Arab Development Aid and the New Dynamics of Multilateralism: Towards Better Governance. *European Scientific Journal*, 10(1), pp. 591–604.

UAE Ministry of Foreign Affairs & International Cooperation, 2021. *Development Assistance*. [Online] Available at: https://www.mofaic.gov.ae/en/the-ministry/the-foreign-policy/development-assistance

UAE Ministry of International Cooperation and Development, 2013. *United Arab Emirates Foreign Aid 2013*, Abu Dhabi: UAE Ministry of International Cooperation and Development.

UNICEF, 2021. *Yemen Humanitarian Situation Report*. New York: UNICEF. [Online] Available at: https://reliefweb.int/report/yemen/unicef-yemen-humanitarian-situation-report-reporting-period-1-30-november-2021-enar

USAID, 2021a. *Promote*. [Online] Available at: https://www.usaid.gov/afghanistan/promote

USAID, 2021b. *Sudan - Complex Emergency*. Washington, DC: USAID. [Online] Available at: https://www.usaid.gov/sites/default/files/documents/08.16.2021_-_USG_Sudan_Complex_Emergency_Fact_Sheet_4.pdf

USAID, 2022. *Gender Equality and Women's Empowerment*. [Online] Available at: https://www.usaid.gov/what-we-do/gender-equality-and-womens-empowerment#:~:text=In%20March%202021%2C%20President%20Biden,our%20Nation%20and%20of%20the

USAID Office of Press Relations, 2021. *Sudan*. [Online] Available at: https://www.usaid.gov/humanitarian-assistance/sudan

US Department of the Treasury, 2021. *Statement from Treasury on Heavily Indebted Poor Countries Debt Relief for Sudan*. [Online] Available at: https://home.treasury.gov/news/press-releases/jy0250#:~:text=WASHINGTON%20%E2%80%94%20The%20U.S.%20Department%20of,debt%20relief%20under%20the%20Heavily

US Government Accoutability Office, 2020. *Progress Is Stalled over Nonproliferation Conditions and Agency Management of Negotiations Is Unclear*. Washington DC: GAO. [Online] Available at: https://www.gao.gov/assets/gao-20-343.pdf

van der Linde, H. and Pomeroy, J., 2021. *Africa's demographics: Young, urban, and eager to work*. London: HSBC. [Online] Available at: https://www.southsuez.com/wp-content/uploads/2021/09/Africas-demographics-HSBC-Sep21.pdf

Villanger, E., 2007. *Arab Foreign Aid: Disbursement Patterns, Aid Policies and Motives*. Bergen: Chr. Michelsen Institute.

Waal, A. de, 2019. *Sudan: A Political Marketplace Framework Analysis*. Occasional Paper No. 19, World Peace Foundation. [Online] Available at: https://sites.tufts.edu/reinventingpeace/files/2019/07/Sudan-A-political-market-place-analysis-final-20190731.pdf

Walsh, J., 2021. *U.S. Cuts Off $700 Million In Aid To Sudan Amid Military Coup.* [Online] Available at: https://www.forbes.com/sites/joewalsh/2021/10/25/us-cuts-off-700-million-in-aid-to-sudan-amid-military-coup/?sh=449ffc1e6637

WAM, 2021. *UAE announces $10 billion fund for investments in Israel.* [Online] Available at: https://gulfnews.com/uae/government/uae-announces-10-billion-fund-for-investments-in-israel-1.1615487088514

Watson Institute, 2021. *Costs of War.* [Online] Available at: https://watson.brown.edu/costsofwar/figures/2021/human-and-budgetary-costs-date-us-war-afghanistan-2001-2022

Weber, A., 2019. *For a Peaceful Transition in Sudan.* Berlin: Stiftung Wissenschaft und Politik (SWP), German Institute for International and Security Affairs.

Woertz, E., 2020. Wither the Self-sufficiency Illusion? Food Security in Arab Gulf States and the Impact of COVID-19. *Food Security*, 12, pp. 757–760.

Woertz, E., 2021. When "Pariahs" Go Green: Energy Transitions in the Middle East and the Biden Administration. *Georgetown Journal of International Affairs.* [Online] Available at: https://gjia.georgetown.edu/2021/04/14/when-pariahs-go-green-energy-transitions-in-the-middle-east-and-the-biden-administration/

Woetzel, J., Garemo, N., Mischke, J., Hjerpe, M. & Palter, R., 2016. *Bringing Global Infrastructure Gaps.* New York: McKinsey and Co. [Online] Available at: https://www.mckinsey.com/business-functions/operations/our-insights/bridging-global-infrastructure-gaps

World Bank, 2020. *Press Release "Covid-19: Remittance Flows to Shrink 14% by 2021.* [Online] Available at: https://www.worldbank.org/en/news/press-release/2020/10/29/covid-19-remittance-flows-to-shrink-14-by-2021

Xueqing, J., 2019. *BOC unit to ramp up services in Middle East.* [Online] Available at: http://www.chinadaily.com.cn/a/201903/29/WS5c9d85daa3104842260b34a7.html

Yemen Data Project, 2019. *Yemen Data Project.* [Online] Available at: https://mailchi.mp/e60be0e82afa/four_years_of_saudi_uae_coalition_yemen_air_war_first_civilian_casualties_data_released_by_yemen_data_project-492823

Yiu, K., 2019. *Saudi prince's trip to China highlighted by $10 billion petrochemical deal.* [Online] Available at: https://abcnews.go.com/International/saudi-princes-trip-china-highlighted-10-billion-petrochemical/story?id=61233563

Young, K. E., 2013. *The Emerging Interventionists of the GCC.* LSE Middle East Centre Paper Series, #2. [Online] Available at: https://core.ac.uk/download/pdf/18581929.pdf

Young, K. E., 2014. *The Political Economy of the United Arab Emirates: Finance, Energy and Security (Between the Majilis and the Market).* New York: Palgrave.

Young, K. E., 2016a. *The Arab Gulf States Institute in Washington.* [Online] Available at: https://agsiw.org/failing-gulf-megafirms-leave-workers-broke-and-stranded/

Young, K. E., 2016b. *The Gulf's Entanglement in Egypt.* [Online] Available at: https://agsiw.org/the-gulfs-entanglement-in-egypt/

Young, K. E., 2017a. A New Politics of GCC Economic Statecraft: The Case of UAE Aid and Financial Intervention in Egypt. *Journal of Arabian Studies*, 7, pp. 113–136.

Young, K. E., 2017b. *Oman's Fiscal Management Problem.* [Online] Available at: https://agsiw.org/omans-fiscal-management-problem/

Young, K. E., 2017c. *Self-Imposed Barriers to Economic Integration in the GCC.* [Online] Available at: https://agsiw.org/self-imposed-barriers-economic-integration-gcc/

Young, K. E., 2018a. *Game on: The new politics of Gulf financial intervention.* [Online] Available at: https://www.aei.org/economics/international-economics/game-on-the-new-politics-of-gulf-financial-intervention/ [Accessed 15 September 2021].

Young, K. E., 2018b. *Master Developers: The New Sino-Arab Gulf Visions of Economic Development.* [Online] Available at: https://www.lawfareblog.com/master-developers-new-sino-arab-gulf-visions-economic-development

Young, K. E., 2018c. *Oman's Investment and Reform Strategy: "Slow and Go".* [Online] Available at: https://agsiw.org/omans-investment-and-reform-strategy-slow-and-go/

Young, K. E., 2019. *The Gulf's Eastward Turn: The Logic of Gulf-China Economic Ties.* [Online] Available at: https://www.aei.org/research-products/report/the-gulfs-eastward-turn-the-logic-of-gulf-china-economic-ties/

Young, K. E., 2020a. *China is Not the Middle East's High Roller.* [Online] Available at: https://www.bloomberg.com/opinion/articles/2020-07-02/china-is-not-the-middle-east-s-high-roller?sref=euelgVQS

Young, K. E., 2020b. *Gulf Arab States Should Make the Most of Oil's Last Boom.* [Online] Available at: https://www.bloomberg.com/opinion/articles/2021-03-12/gulf-states-should-make-the-most-of-oil-s-last-boom?sref=euelgVQS [Accessed 21 September 2021].

Young, K. E., 2020c. *The reboot: American leadership in the post-COVID global economy.* [Online] Available at: https://www.aei.org/foreign-and-defense-policy/the-reboot-american-leadership-in-the-post-covid-global-economy/

Young, K., 2020d. Twin Policy Crises Deepen Gulf States' Policy Competition and Independence. *Global Discourse*, 10(4), pp. 481–487.

Young, K. E., 2020e. *Banks can't save Gulf economies.* [Online] Available at: https://www.al-monitor.com/originals/2020/04/gcc-economy-covid19-coronavirus-banks-save.html

Young, K. E., 2021a. *Israel's Abraham Accords Dividend Is in Doubt.* [Online] Available at: https://www.bloomberg.com/opinion/articles/2021-05-25/after-gaza-israel-s-abraham-accords-dividend-is-in-doubt

Young, K. E., 2021b. *The Middle East and the Global Energy Transition.* [Online] Available at: https://www.mei.edu/publications/middle-east-and-global-energy-transition

Zawya, 2021a. *Egypt to increase price of subsidized vegetable oil - minister.* [Online] Available at: https://www.zawya.com/saudi-arabia/en/markets/story/Egypt_to_increase_price_of_subsidized_vegetable_oil__minister-TR20211028nC6N2R002KX4/

Zawya, 2021b. *PROJECTS: Morocco aims for 100% renewable energy sufficiency.* [Online] Available at: https://www.zawya.com/mena/en/projects/story/PROJECTS_Morocco_aims_for_100_renewable_energy_sufficiency-ZAWYA20210121074012/

Zunes, S., 2021. *Sudan's 2019 Revolution: The Power of Cicvil Resistance.* ICNC Special Report Series #5. [Online] Available at: https://www.nonviolent-conflict.org/wp-content/uploads/2021/04/Zunes-Sudans-2019-Revolution.pdf

INDEX

NOTE: Page numbers followed by a letter 'f' or 't' indicate figures or tables, respectively.

patterns of intervention 127
regional influence and investment
2–6, 18, 21–2, 34, 129
twin crises response 26–31
See also Gulf-China synergy;
oil-based economies; specific
countries
Gulf-China synergy
competition within MENA 38–9
economic ties 34–9
energy infrastructure projects
32
finance sector and 32–3
financial intervention and 42
infrastructure projects 31–4
roles as regional investors 3–4,
8–9, 21

Haitham bin Tariq Al Said 96, 100
Harari, Yuval Noah 17
Henderson, Christian 110
Hill, Ginny 124, 127
Horn of Africa
food security 110, 113
Gulf influence in 68–70
strategic location 48, 68–70
Houthis. *See* Yemen
Humphrey, C., 41

IMF (International Monetary Fund).
See bilateral and multilateral
funding
immigration policy 27, 30–1
inflation 51, 71, 76, 135
infrastructure investment
demand for 5, 43
Gulf-China synergy and 31–4
See also specific countries
investment. *See* financial intervention
Iran
Gulf tensions with 119–20
Pakistan relations with 89, 90, 91
US tensions with 98
Islamic Development Bank (IsDB)
43–4
Israel 103f, 117–19

Jinko Solar (China) 32
jobs. *See* labor force
Jordan 33, 102f, 103f, 135

Khalifa Fund for Enterprise
Development (UAE) 74
Kicking Away the Ladder (Chang) 141
Kuwait 23–4, 53, 54, 55f
Kuwait Fund for Development 44, 54

labor force
foreign workers in Gulf 30–1
job creation and foreign aid 56
60–1
Pakistanis in Saudi Arabia 90–1
twin crises and demographics of
28, 30, 31
women in 23, 28, 30, 48, 122–3
youth in 28, 79, 122
See also specific countries
lending. *See* development aid;
financial intervention
liberalism, role of 17. *See also*
political economy of
development
Lipset, Seymour Martin 15
liquefied natural gas (LNG). *See*
energy resources and
production
Litan, David 9–10

Mackenzie, Baker 17–18
magic decade (2003-2014) 26, 50, 67.
See also oil prices
Majid al Futtaim group (UAE) 67
Marubeni Corporation (Japan) 32
McCartney, M., 90
Mexico, partnership with OPEC 25
MIGA (Multilateral Investment
Guarantee Agency, World
Bank) 85
migrants. *See* labor force
militaries
financial aid and training 12, 38,
50
intervention 6, 11

political economy compared with
Oman 85
reliance on foreign aid 86
remittance flows into 84–5, 88
Saudi ties with 90–1
World Bank assessment of 88
Yemen conflict and 91
PetroChina 32
petroleum. *See* energy resources and
production; magic decade
(2003-2014); oil prices;
oil-based economies
political economy of development
13–20
authoritarian capitalism 2, 10
Bahrain *vs.* Kuwait 23–4
challenges of multipolarity 10–12
Chinese initiatives 17–18
democracy 15, 16–17
Gulf state initiatives 18–19
institutional pathways and
incentives 15–16
liberalism 17
trends in aid models 13–14, 18–20
Pottinger, Matt 11–12
Power, Samantha 115
Public Investment Fund (Saudi
Arabia) 29, 32

Qatar
energy sector 66
finance sector weaknesses 29
foreign aid and investments of 54,
79f, 102f, 117f
GCC dispute and blockade of
24–5, 57, 59, 83, 98
infrastructure development 35
reliance on LNG 58, 59

real estate sector 51, 58, 75, 80. *See
also* specific countries
reconstruction. *See* conflict
environments
regional security, as motivation for
investment 69–70. *See also*
militaries

remittance flows. *See* specific
countries
renewable energy. *See* energy
resources and production
rents and rent-seeking behavior 15,
21, 50, 55–6, 109
Robinson, James 15–16
Rondos, Alex 19
rule-based economic systems 14
Russia, partnership with OPEC 25, 137

Sabri, Nidal 44
SAMA (Saudi Central Bank) 29, 136
SANED program (Saudi Arabia) 138
Saudi Arabia
austerity and crisis recovery 28,
29–30
Chinese investment in 32, 33, 36
Covid response 138
energy sector 32, 91, 133, 140
foreign aid and investment of 40,
54, 55f, 102f, 116f
government debt 26
institutionalization of aid agencies
122
oil price decline effects on 25, 55f
Pakistan ties with 90–1
Vision 2030 29
Saudi Central Bank (SAMA) 29, 136
Saudi Development and
Reconstruction Program for
Yemen (SDRPY) 122, 123f
Saudi Public Investment Fund 78
Scissors, Derek 17
security institutions. *See* military
shale revolution (2014)
Covid pandemic and 137
oil prices and 25–6, 56, 67
See also twin crises
Sharia compliant investment 51, 66
Sharif, Raheel 91
Sheikh Tahnoon bin Zayed al
Nayhan 75, 113
al-Sisi, Abdel Fatah 45, 80
solar energy. *See* energy resources
and production